THE PASSIONATE PRAYER NOTEBOOK

CATHERINE MARTIN

THE
PASSIONATE
PRAYER
NOTEBOOK

QuietTime
MINISTRIES

PALM DESERT, CALIFORNIA

The Passionate Prayer Notebook
Copyright © 2013 by Catherine Martin
Published by Quiet Time Ministries
Palm Desert, California 92255
www.quiettime.org

ISBN-13: 978-0-9766886-8-6

Second Edition published by Quiet Time Ministries 2013

Printed in the United States of America
13 14 15 16 17 18 19 20 21/ ACS / 11 10 9 8 7 6 5 4 3 2

EX LIBRIS

_____

Dates

_____

_____

My Key Word & Verse

_____

_____

Don't worry about anything, instead pray about everything…
PHILIPPIANS 4:6 NLT

———

I urge you, first of all, to pray…
1 TIMOTHY 2:1 NLT

———

With all prayer and petition pray at all times in the Spirit, and with this in view, be on the alert with all perseverance and petition for all the saints…
EPHESIANS 6:18 NASB

———

The world is full of observers. Every now and then, some people step out of the crowd, hear the music of the Lord, and respond, becoming active participants with Him. They walk and talk with God, engaging in lives of prayer. They share in the Lord's life, and He shares in their lives. The music comes from the Lord, through His Word applied by the Holy Spirit, constantly asking you to open the door of your life to walk and talk with Him. And when you walk and talk with Him, you pray— passionately and from the heart.
CATHERINE MARTIN, PASSIONATE PRAYER—A 30 DAY JOURNEY

———

❧ CONTENTS ❧

ᴥ INTRODUCTION ᴥ

One of the greatest privileges God has given us is prayer. To be able to run to our Lord at any time and talk with Him is absolutely incredible. I often think about the blind beggar, Bartimaeus. He heard that Jesus was close by and cried out to Him for mercy. Jesus responded to him by asking, "what do you want Me to do for you" (Mark 10:51). Oh those words are just music to the ears of every child of God. Imagine, Jesus is asking you, dear friend, "what do you want Me to do for you?" He healed Bartimaeus and gave him his sight. What will He do for you if only you will pray?

I want to ask you, "How's your life of prayer these days? Do you pray?" I think about the woman who was talking with a friend about how difficult her life was. She said, "I've done everything I can do. All that's left is prayer." Her friend replied, "Oh dear, has it come to that!" We laugh, but sometimes, we act as though prayer is our last resort, rather than our first action when we are in trouble. Paul told his disciple, Timothy, "I urge you, first of all, to pray…" (1 Timothy 2:1 NLT). Prayer should always be the first response in our lives.

God wants us pray. I find that truth to be so wonderful that I can hardly keep it to myself. Listen to these words in Hebrews 4:15-16 and get excited: "For we do not have a high priest who cannot sympathize with our weaknesses, but One who has been tempted in all things as we are, yet without sin. Therefore, let us draw near with confidence to the throne of grace, so that we may receive mercy and find grace to help in time of need." Do you sense the power in those words? The truth that God is inviting me into His throne room to receive mercy and find grace in my need drives me deeper into prayer, even now.

I remember early in my relationship with the Lord reading *How To Pray* by R.A. Torrey. In that book, Torrey wrote:

> Mercy is what we need, grace is what we must have, or all our life and effort will end in complete failure. Prayer is the way to get them. There is infinite grace at our disposal, and we make it ours experimentally by prayer. Oh, if we only realized the fullness of God's grace that is ours for the asking, its height and depth and length and breadth, I am sure we would spend more time in prayer. The measure of our appropriation of grace is determined by the measure of our prayers…what little streams of mercy and grace most of us know, when we might know rivers overflowing their banks…By prayer the bitterest enemies of the Gospel have become its most valiant defenders, the greatest scoundrels the truest sons of God, and the vilest women the purest saints. Oh, the power of prayer to reach down,

down, down where hope itself seems vain, and lift men and women up, up, up into fellowship with and likeness to God.[1]

Torrey continued by writing that God is listening for the voice of prayer. Then, he asked: "Will He hear it? Will He hear it from you? Will He hear it from the church as a body?"[2] Then, as if to answer all his questions, he wrote, "I believe He will." Next to those words I wrote, "Amen!" And I meant it with all my heart. I remember being so excited at what God taught me in Torrey's book that I was reading paragraphs from it to my friends. Oh how I longed to be someone who didn't just talk about prayer. I wanted to be someone who actually prayed.

Over the years I have given great thought to my own life of prayer. I've asked, "So do I pray? And how is my life of prayer?" I remember one day in particular asking myself those questions again after reading some powerful verses in the Bible about prayer. As a result, I decided to get serious and intentional, and become passionate about prayer.

Passionate prayer is prayer from the heart. Passionate prayer takes you on an exciting adventure of conversation and communion from your heart to the heart of God. My goal for you is that your prayer life displays the powerful and compelling emotions of infinite love for God and boundless enthusiasm for prayer as a discipline. I see a life of passionate prayer as singing sweet music to the ears of the Lord. I see passionate prayer deepening your relationship with God through a prayer growth plan that can be individualized just for you. I see passionate prayer modeled from the wisdom of heroes of the faith and Jesus Himself. I see passionate prayer prevailing through the promises of God. I see passionate prayer empowering revival, intercession, and spiritual warfare.

Bill Bright used to tell this story:

A man traveled to a certain city one cold morning. As he arrived at his hotel, he noticed that the clerks, the guests—everyone—was barefoot. In the coffee shop, he noticed a fellow at a nearby table and asked, "Why aren't you wearing shoes? Don't you know about shoes?"

"Of course I know about shoes," the patron replied.

"Then why don't you wear them?" The visitor asked.

"Ah, that is the question," the patron returned. "Why don't I wear shoes?"

After breakfast, the visitor walked out of the hotel and into the snow. Again, every person he saw was barefoot. Curious, he asked a passerby, "Why doesn't anyone here wear shoes? Don't you know that they protect the feet from cold?"

The passerby said, "We know about shoes. See that building? It's a shoe factory. We are so proud of the plant that we gather there every week to hear the man in charge tell us how wonderful shoes are."

"Then why don't you wear shoes?" the visitor persisted.

"Ah, that is the question," the passerby replied. "Why don't we wear shoes?"

Bill Bright would then explain that when it comes to prayer, many Christians are like the people in that city. They know about prayer, they believe in its power, and they frequently hear sermons on the subject, but it is not a vital part of their lives.

I want to ask you, "Have you discovered the great adventure of passionate prayer? Is prayer a vital part of your life? Would you like to be the kind of man or woman who takes everything to the Lord in prayer and sees Him do great and mighty things in their lives as a result? Do you long to engage more deeply in the great adventure of knowing your God?

You hold in your hands some of the fruit of what God has been teaching me about prayer over the course of many years, *The Passionate Prayer Notebook*. Over the years, I've used the Passionate Prayer Notebook pages, drawing me deeper into a life of passionate prayer, and teaching me more and more how pray. I look at prayer as a lifetime journey where we grow deeper and more passionate in walking and talking with God. Through intention and purpose and planning, we can grow in prayer. The *Passionate Prayer Notebook* contains pages for your own Prayer Growth Plan. These are the pages that I love the most and have found to be especially effective and life-changing. These pages include:

- Prayer Journal

- Scripture Prayer

- Listening To God

- Thank You, Lord

- Quotes on Prayer

- Books on Prayer

- Adventure in Prayer

- Knowing God

- ACTS Prayer

- Prayer Focus

These pages can be used in many ways as you spend time with the Lord in your quiet time. They are a place for you to write out your prayers. There is space for you to write insights, observations, thoughts, prayers, and any other practical applications that God works into your life from your time in His Word as you grow in your life of prayer.

I've excerpted chapters from my book, *Passionate Prayer—A 30 Day Journey*, to help get you started in growing in your prayer life using *The Passionate Prayer Notebook*. I've included instructions and examples. The exciting part is that not only will you study and learn more about prayer, you have a resource that will help you immediately apply what you are learning and pray more passionately, from the heart.

The Passionate Prayer Notebook is designed to be a resource for you in your quiet time. And when its pages are filled, you will have a testimony in written form of all that God is teaching you about prayer. You will notice there is a place at the front of *The Passionate Prayer Notebook* for you to write your name, the dates, and a key verse. You may use more than one *Passionate Prayer Notebook* in a year, and these notebooks will be chronicles of your adventure with the Lord as you grow in your knowledge of Him.

So dear friend, will you set aside the many things for the one thing in life, the great pursuit of knowing God? Someday you will stand face to face with your Lord. I want you to be able to look into eyes that are familiar to you because you have spent much time with Him now. I want you to enjoy His beauty and experience His love. When you are face to face with Him, you will know that your time alone with Him in prayer was worth it all. God bless you, dear friend, as you engage in the great adventure of knowing Him.

QUIET TIME MINISTRIES ONLINE

Quiet Time Ministries Online at www.quiettime.org is a place where you can deepen your devotion to God and His Word. Cath's Blog is where Catherine shares about life, about the Lord, and just about everything else. A Walk In Grace™ is Catherine's devotional photojournal, highlighting her own photography, where you can grow deep in the garden of His grace. Quiet Time Ministries proudly sponsors Ministry For Women at www.ministryforwomen.com—a social network community for women worldwide to grow in their relationship with Jesus Christ. Connect, study, and grow at Ministry For Women. Quiet Time Ministries proudly sponsors Catherine Martin's myPhotoWalk at www.myphotowalk.com where lovers of photography can experience the great adventure of knowing God through Devotional Photography.

MY LETTER TO THE LORD

As you begin using *The Passionate Prayer Notebook*, I'd like to ask, where are you? What has been happening in your life over the last year or so? What has been your life experience? What are you facing and what has God been teaching you? It is no accident that you have *The Passionate Prayer Notebook* to use in your quiet time. In fact, God has something He wants you to know, something that will change the whole landscape of your experience with Him. Watch for it, listen for it, and when you learn it, write it down and never let it go. Will you write a prayer in the form of a letter to the Lord in the space provided expressing all that is on your heart and ask Him to speak to you as you draw near and grow in your life of passionate prayer with Him?

MY LETTER TO THE LORD

THE PASSIONATE PRAYER GUIDE

YOUR SONG TO THE LORD

Be filled with the Spirit. Speak to one another with psalms, hymns and spiritual
songs. Sing and make music in your heart to the Lord, always giving thanks
to God the Father for everything, in the name of our Lord Jesus Christ.
EPHESIANS 5:18-20

Prayer is your song to the Lord in response to His presence in your life. The psalmists knew the response of prayer as a song. Again and again they wrote words like these:

"I will sing to the LORD" (Psalm 13:6).
"He put a new song in my mouth" (Psalm 40:3).

"I will remember my song in the night, I will meditate with my heart, and my spirit ponders" (Psalm 77:6).

"Sing to the Lord a new song" (Psalm 96:1).

"The LORD is my strength and song" (Psalm 118:14).

"Your statutes are my songs" (Psalm 119:54).

"I will sing a new song to You, O God" (Psalm 144:9).

"Bless the LORD, O my soul! O LORD my God, You are very great; You are clothed wit splendor and majesty…I will sing to the LORD as long as I live; I will sing praise to my God while I have my being" (Psalm 104:1,33).

You may speak the words of your song of prayer. You may hum the thoughts in your heart and mind. Or you may literally sing your prayer out loud to the Lord. However you walk and talk with the Lord, your prayer is likened to a melody in your heart directed to your Lord. Paul said, "Be filled with the Spirit. Speak to one another with psalms, hymns and spiritual songs. Sing and make music in your heart to the Lord, always giving thanks to God the Father for everything, in the name of our Lord Jesus Christ" (Ephesians 5:18-20 NIV). J.B. Phillips translates this verse to read, "Let the Spirit stimulate your souls. Express your joy in singing among yourselves psalms and hymns and spiritual songs, making music in your hearts for the ears of God!" I love that translation, for prayer is the voice that reaches the audience of God Himself. God prompts your prayers, empowers your prayers, and hears your prayers.

Why do we pray? There are five principle reasons: the *call* from God, *consecration* to God, *communion* with God, *conversation* with God, and *cooperation* with God.

First, prayer is our calling from God—it's how we obey God. He doesn't just ask us to pray, He commands us! "Pray without ceasing" (1 Thessalonians 5:17). In fact, the Bible assumes prayer in our lives. God conversed with Adam in the garden (Genesis 3:9-12). Jesus used the phrase "when you pray" at least three times, assuming that we *will* pray (Matthew 6:5-7). The very existence and being of God commands a response from us, thus making prayer an imperative.

Second, prayer is our consecration to God—it's how we commit ourselves to Him. Our devotion to God is seen in our prayers to Him. Throughout the psalms you will notice this great resolve to pray:

"I will give thanks to the Lord with all my heart" (Psalm 9:1).
"In the morning I will order my prayer to You and eagerly watch" (Psalm 5:3).

"I will cry to God Most High, to God who accomplishes all things for me" (Psalm 57:2).

"Evening and morning and at noon I will pray, and cry aloud, and He shall hear my voice" (Psalm 55:17 NKJV).

Third, prayer is communion with God—it's how we walk with Him. God's desire for intimacy is not only written in His Word but also imprinted on our hearts through the indwelling Holy Spirit. Paul says, "For you have not received a spirit of slavery leading to fear again, but you have received a spirit of adoption as sons by which we cry out, 'Abba! Father!' The Spirit Himself testifies with our spirit that we are children of God" (Romans 8:15-16).

Fourth, prayer is our conversation with God—it's how we talk with Him. He talks with us in His Word, and we must respond if there is to be a two-way conversation. Our response to God is prayer. You discover this response and learn about prayer throughout Scripture itself. Many of the psalms are prayers and provide examples of how to pray. The psalmist said, "The LORD will command His lovingkindness in the daytime; and His song will be with me in the night, a prayer to the God of my life" (Psalm 42:8).

Finally, prayer is our cooperation with God—it's how we serve with God. When we pray, we join in ministry with the Lord. For reasons known only to God Himself, He has chosen to include us in His work by responding to our prayers and carrying out His plans and purposes.

David expressed this amazing power of prayer to the Lord when he said, "I waited patiently for the LORD; and He inclined to me and heard my cry" (Psalm 40:1). Oswald Chambers says, "Prayer does not fit us for the greater works; prayer *is* the greater work."[1] Throughout the Bible, you will notice that when God's people prayed, God responded with supernatural, extraordinary power. (Read about Moses on Mt. Sinai in Exodus 33:18-23, Gideon and the Midianites in Judges 6–7, and Hezekiah and the Assyrians in 2 Kings 19.)

I believe God must be utterly shocked when we do not pray. How can I make such a bold statement? Three incidents in the Bible give me this impression about God's surprise at prayer-lessness in the lives of His people.

When the people of God stepped away from Him and lived a life of immorality and oppression, God said, "I searched for a man among them who would build up the wall and stand in the gap before Me for the land, so that I would not destroy it; but I found no one" (Ezekiel 22:30).

I remember hearing a message on these words from Ezekiel many years ago and was profoundly moved to realize that God spent time looking for someone to pray for His people and found no one. I thought to myself, *Well, even if no one else is willing, I want to step up to the plate and pray for others so that the next time God is looking for someone, His eyes might rest on me.*

In Isaiah 65:1-2, God speaks about the rebellion of His people:

> I permitted Myself to be sought by those who did not ask for Me; I permitted Myself to be found by those who did not seek Me. I said, "Here am I, here am I," to a nation which did not call on My name. I have spread out My hands all day long to a rebellious people, who walk in the way which is not good, following their own thoughts.

In these verses, I see that God notices when I do not pray. I see the open and wounded heart of God, who is calling out to His people. These words embarrass me if I will not pray. To know that God is calling out to me for a relationship and yet to remain prayerless, to never talk with Him, is a sad estate that we must not allow in our lives.

Finally, I love the example of Samuel, who knew God and His view of prayer. On one occasion when the people were in danger from the Philistines, Samuel said, "Gather all Israel to Mizpah and I will pray to the LORD for you" (1 Samuel 7:5). The people begged Samuel, "Do not cease to cry to the LORD our God for us, that He may save us from the hand of the Philistines" (1 Samuel 7:8). God delivered the people in answer to Samuel's prayer. Then, when the people of God realized they had offended God by asking for a king, the people said to Samuel, "Pray for your servants to the LORD your God, so that we may not die, for we have added to all our sins this evil by asking for ourselves a king" (1 Samuel 12:19). Samuel's response reveals his understanding of prayer: "As for me, far be it from me that I should sin against the LORD by ceasing to pray for you; but I will instruct you in the good and right way" (1 Samuel 12:23). Samuel understood God's expectation of prayer in our lives. God wants this intimate sharing of our life and expects us to walk with Him and talk with Him about everything.

E.M. Bounds says, "Prayer moves the hand that moves the world." There can be no doubt that prayer makes a difference to God. You can know that when you pray, something powerful is going to happen. When Israel cried out to God in their suffering, God "looked upon their distress when He heard their cry; and He remembered His covenant for their sake, and relented according to the greatness of His lovingkindness. He also made them objects of compassion in the presence of all their captors" (Psalm 106:44-46). God relented concerning the calamity awaiting Ninevah when the people called earnestly upon God for forgiveness (Jonah 3:8-10). James clearly shows the significance of your prayers when he says, "You do not have because you do not ask" (James 4:2). According to James, "The effective prayer of a righteous man can accomplish much" (James 5:16).

In all these examples, we see the power of one prayer to our God. One prayer makes a difference with God and can ultimately impact people and nations. Always remember, God is looking for the one who will pray. May He find you and me offering that one prayer.

The Bible constantly teaches us about prayer and gives us numerous examples of prayer.

God is moved by our prayers (2 Samuel 24:25).

God listens to our prayers (1 Kings 8:28).

There are many postures for prayer, including kneeling and spreading our hands upward toward God (1 Kings 8:54).

God relieves distress in answer to prayer (Psalm 4:1).

We can pray out loud to the Lord (Psalm 5:3).

We should pray and then eagerly watch to see what God will do (Psalm 5:3).

We should pray when we are afflicted and needy (Psalm 86:1).

The psalmists often prayed in the morning (Psalm 5:3; 88:13).

God hears the prayers of the destitute (Psalm 102:17).

Prayer is like incense before the Lord (Psalm 141:2).

God delights in our prayers (Proverbs 15:8).

God hears our prayers and sees our tears (Isaiah 38:5).

We seek the Lord by prayer and supplications (Daniel 9:3).

Prayer is an act of devotion (Acts 6:4).

Prayer is a memorial to the Lord (Acts 10:4).

Fervent prayer accomplishes much (Acts 12:5).

We should pray for the salvation of others (Romans 10:1).

We are to be devoted to prayer (Romans 12:12).

We are to pray at all times in the Spirit (Ephesians 6:18).

Prayer should be given with an attitude of thanksgiving (Colossians 4:2).

Prayer includes entreaties, prayers, petitions, and thanksgiving for all men (1 Timothy 2:1).

We should pray night and day (1 Timothy 5:5).

Sometimes prayer is offered to God with loud crying and tears to God (Hebrews 5:7).

Prayer is to be offered in faith (James 5:15).

Your prayer can accomplish much (James 5:16).

We are to pray about everything (Philippians 4:6-7).

Constant prayer is the alternative to losing heart (Luke 18:1).

We are to pray according to God's will (1 John 5:14-15).

We are to pray without ceasing (1 Thessalonians 5:17).

Prayer in secret brings reward from your Father (Matthew 6:6).

We should often slip away to a quiet place and pray (Luke 5:16).

Prayer gives you spiritual strength (Luke 21:36).

The Spirit helps us pray in our weakness (Romans 8:26).

When you suffer, you should pray (James 5:13).

This list is not exhaustive, but these many principles about prayer taught in the Bible demonstrate how important prayer is to God and to us. Paul implores us to make the most of our time because the days are evil (Ephesians 5:16). One of the ways we use our time wisely is to pray.

In the early 1870s, not long after the disastrous Chicago fire, D.L. Moody traveled from Chicago to London while waiting for his church to be rebuilt. He spent his time listening to Spurgeon and other preachers. One day he attended a meeting in Exeter Hall on the Strand, and when visiting preachers were invited to share, Moody responded. After the meeting, a minister invited Moody to his church to preach the next morning and evening.

> I went to the morning service and found a large church full of people. And when the time came, I began to speak to them. But it seemed the hardest talking I ever did. There was no response in their faces. They seemed as though carved out of stone or ice. And I was having a hard time: and I wished I wasn't there; and wished I hadn't promised to speak again at night. But I had promised, and so I went.

That evening, Moody experienced the same lack of response in the beginning of his preaching. Then he describes an amazing occurrence:

> About half-way through my talk there came a change. It seemed as thought the windows of heaven had opened and a bit of breath blew down. The atmosphere of the building seemed to change. The people's faces changed. It impressed me so that when I finished speaking I gave the invitation for those who wanted to be Christians to rise. I thought there might be a few. And to my immense surprise the people got up in groups.

He preached for ten days to packed audiences, and more than four hundred people were added to that church. All the churches in the area were affected by Moody's preaching. Because of that experience, Moody realized his life work of preaching in areas beyond his own church, known as his "roving commission," marking the beginning of what we know as evangelistic crusades.[2]

Moody wondered about the explanation of the dramatic change in the church as he was preaching that first evening. He set out to discover the secret and was rewarded for his efforts. A woman who was a member of the church had become sick and was told by her physician that she would not recover but would be shut in her home for years. She lay there wondering what a life in bed for years would mean for her. She thought, *How little I've done for God: practically nothing: and now what can I do shut in here on my back?* And she thought, *I can pray.* And then, *I will pray.*

And so she prayed for her church. Her sister who lived with her gave her reports about the church. One Sunday at noon after church, her sister went into her room and said, "Who do you think preached today? A stranger from America, a man called Moody, I think was the name."

The sick woman's face turned white, her lip trembled, and she quietly said, "I know what that means. There's something coming to the old church. Don't bring me any dinner. I must spend this afternoon in prayer." And that night, God moved in a powerful way in the church.

When Moody visited this woman, she told him how two years before she had received a Chicago paper with one of Moody's sermons. When she read it, her heart burned, and she was led to pray that God would send Moody to their church. Just a simple prayer from a simple woman known by no one. She prayed for two years. And God brought Moody from Chicago to London to her church. All this was in answer to the prayer of a woman who dared to ask God for something only He could do. God loves a prayer like that. May we join her great company and dare to pray for extraordinary things and watch eagerly to see what God will do as we walk and talk with Him.

WHEN YOU FINALLY SING

Therefore repent and return, so that your sins may be wiped away, in order that times of refreshing may come from the presence of the Lord.
ACTS 3:19

Prayer changes you. When you walk and talk with the Lord, you are transformed by His very presence. In Acts 3:19, Peter encourages his listeners to repent so that "times of refreshing may come from the presence of the Lord." Jesus says that when you come to Him, you will find "rest for your souls" (Matthew 11:29). The Greek word translated "refreshing" is *anapsuxis,* alluding to a cooling as with a refreshing rain in the summer heat. When you are refreshed and rested, your spiritual life grows. You are moved to pray for others. You find a new peace in a difficult situation. And you trust God for His work in your life. Eugene Peterson says, "We become what we are called to be by praying."[1] A.C. Dixon, the great preacher and pastor of Chicago's famous Moody Church in the early 1900s, declared, "When we rely upon organization, we get what organization can do; when we rely upon education, we get what education can do; when we rely upon eloquence, we get what eloquence can do…but when we rely upon prayer, we get what God can do."

Oh, how our present generation needs to step away from the life of hurry and find the rhythm of walking and talking with Jesus. Most of the time when someone asks how we are doing, our response of "fine" really means, as one movie script put it, Freaked out, Insecure, Neurotic, and Emotional. But when we pray and move in the pace and rhythm of Jesus with pauses, periods, and rests, then our "fine" becomes Faithful, Inspired, Nourished, and Empowered. Faithful to God, inspired by Him, nourished by the Word, and empowered by the Holy Spirit. When we pray, the world can see the change in who we are and what we do.

And so, enriching our lives of prayer is worth the time and energy in order to move into that new rhythm that helps us to finally sing to the Lord. David, the man after God's own heart, discovered this truth when he was in the depth of despair. He was chased by Saul relentlessly for years, yet David possessed the promise to be the future king of Israel. Seeing no fruition of such a tremendous promise from God and forced to escape into enemy territory to flee Saul, David became discouraged. He cried out to God, "How long, O LORD? Will You forget me forever? How long will You hide Your face from me?" (Psalm 13:1).

Have you ever felt completely abandoned by the Lord? If so, then follow David's example. Cry out to God in prayer. That's exactly what David did. And David's prayer led him to trust in the lovingkindness of God. The transformation of David's demeanor is discovered in his subsequent words: "My heart shall rejoice in your salvation. I will sing to the LORD, because He has dealt bountifully with me" (Psalm 13:5-6). When you finally sing in prayer, you will be transformed.

Jean Giono, a French author, was mountain climbing in the French Alps in 1913 and was shocked to find barren mountains because of careless deforestation. Villages were abandoned because of dry brooks and springs. Giono happened upon a shepherd's hut, where he was invited to spend the night. He watched the shepherd sort through a pile of acorns, discarding any that were damaged or unusable. He learned that over the last three years, the shepherd had planted 100,000 trees with those acorns, resulting in 20,000 that actually sprouted. Years later, Giono visited the shepherd again and discovered the new growth of a vast forest as well as bubbling brooks, gardens, and flowers. He returned again after World War II and found the region glowing with health and prosperity. By sorting through piles of acorns and planting trees one day at a time, the shepherd brought new growth, forests, and fresh life.

When you pray, entire regions of your heart and soul and life are dramatically transformed through continuous times of refreshing. You may not notice a change in a day or a week. But wait and watch. You can *eagerly* look for such a renewal, as David says in Psalm 5:3: "In the morning I will order my prayer to You and eagerly watch." Then you'll see what times of refreshing and rest will do in your life. And you will see how the change influences the lives of those around you. Ole Hallesby, a Norwegian theologian, uses this image in his classic book on prayer:

> To pray is nothing more involved than to lie in the sunshine of His grace, to expose our distress of body and soul to those healing rays which can in a wonderful way counteract and render ineffective the bacteria of sin. To be a man or woman of prayer is to take this sun-cure, to give Jesus, with His wonder-working power, access to our distress night and day.[2]

Jesus says that when you walk with Him, you'll recover your life; that is, you'll find "rest for your souls" (Matthew 11:28-30). Do you need that kind of hope today? Then, dear friend, draw near and pray. Ray Stedman says, "Prayer is an awesome, mighty force in the world of men." May that force move in and through you to change the world.

YOUR PRAYER GROWTH PLAN

With all prayer and petition pray at all times in the Spirit, and with this in view, be on the alert with all perseverance and petition for all the saints.

EPHESIANS 6:18

Enriching your life of prayer requires purposeful planning and attention. Moving to a deeper level in the actual practice of prayer necessitates a dedicated time of devotion. While reading through Ephesians 6 in my quiet time, I came to verse 18, and the words *at all times* seemed to flash in neon lights from the page. I firmly believe that when God wants to teach us something in the Word, the Holy Spirit opens our spiritual eyes, highlighting Scripture so we will see its truth for our lives. The eyes of my heart were enlightened (Ephesians 1:18) to see the importance of prayer in my life that day. I read Paul's words as though I had never read them before: "With all prayer and petition pray at all times in the Spirit, and with this in view, be on the alert with all perseverance and petition for all the saints." Do you know what word was most significant to me? A little word with big meaning—*all.* I knew from my pastor at the time that "all means all, and that's all, all means." In one broad brush stroke, the Holy Spirit used this verse to open up my mind and heart to see that I needed to grow deeper and more passionate in my life of prayer. I knew instantly that my life fell far short of such a life of *all* prayer, *all* petition, at *all* times, with *all* perseverance, and for *all* the saints. That little word *all* pointed to passionate prayer. I saw it as a "walking and talking with the Lord" that never stops, flowing from a heart of devotion to God. R.A. Torrey said that when the intelligent child of God stops to weigh the meaning of these words in Ephesians 6:18, he or she is driven to say, "I must pray, pray, pray. I must put all my energy and all my heart into prayer. Whatever else I do, I must pray."[1]

How could I step up to the plate, so to speak, and hit a home run in this new arena of prayer? How could I develop such passionate prayer with power? I made a radical, Holy Spirit–driven decision. I decided to design a prayer growth plan for myself with the guidance of God through His Holy Spirit. The Holy Spirit is the one who guides us in prayer and empowers us from within (Acts 1:8; Romans 8:26-27; Ephesians 5:18). In my case, the Holy Spirit led me to enroll in the school of prayer with serious intent and purpose.

Paul said, "Run in such a way that you may win" (1 Corinthians 9:24). Paul's words encouraged me to seriously consider the steps I take to grow spiritually in my relationship with the Lord. Paul encouraged his disciple Timothy, "Discipline yourself for the purpose of godliness" (1 Timothy 4:7). This level of Pauline discipline is the training necessary for unhindered pursuit of God's purposes. I'm a firm believer in training to be, as Oswald Chambers says, my utmost for His highest. That's one of the reasons why I sought a seminary education. And that's why I just knew, deep in my heart, after reading Ephesians 6:18, I needed a comprehensive prayer growth plan. I wanted to learn how to pray with the same fervor that Jesus' disciples had expressed in their request, "Teach us to pray" (Luke 11:1).

Where was I to begin in developing my prayer growth plan? In developing a life of prayer, I first asked myself these most basic of questions: When would I pray these passionate prayers, where would I pray as Paul described in Ephesians 6:18, and what would be my plan for growth in this life of prayer? I had already established a consistent quiet time by setting aside a time, a place, and a plan, so I already knew the answer to the first question. I realized my growth in prayer would occur best in the context of my quiet time.

To establish a daily quiet time, first set aside a time to be alone with the Lord. The time is best when you are alert and when you can have some uninterrupted moments with your Lord. Jesus often rose early in the morning to pray (Mark 1:35). I prefer the mornings, so that was settled. And then you need a quiet place for a time of communion with the Lord. Organize all your quiet time materials in your quiet place. I like to use a quiet time basket for *The Quiet Time Notebook*, my Bible, devotional reading, prayer helps, worship music, my hymnbook, pencils, pens, and reading glasses. You may have a bookshelf, a file drawer, or a briefcase. It's up to you. To draw near to the Lord each day, I use the P.R.A.Y.E.R. Quiet Time Plan:

Prepare Your Heart

Read and Study God's Word

Adore God in Prayer

Yield Yourself to God

Enjoy His Presence

Rest In His Love[2]

Then I needed to choose a tool to help me grow in this life of passionate prayer. Many years ago, I designed the *The Quiet Time Notebook* to use in my quiet time. Then I revised the *The Quiet*

Time Notebook for others at the outset of Quiet Time Ministries. I have discovered that using a notebook with topical sections is a perfect reminder of all I can do in my quiet time. One of the sections in the *The Quiet Time Notebook* is Adore God in Prayer. I had been using these Adore God in Prayer pages in my notebook to keep a record of my requests and God's answers to my prayers.

I thought, *Now I want to go deeper and focus on specific areas to grow in.* I prayed over a list of considerations: the importance of learning to talk with God, the use of Scripture, the various types of prayers in the Bible, learning from others, writing my own prayers, expressing and tracking my prayer growth, and knowing the character of God. Then I looked to the Bible as my university of prayer with four classrooms that will teach me how to pray: the psalms, the promises, the prayers, and the people. With these ideas in mind I developed the Passionate Prayer Growth Plan—ten new areas to help me grow in my life of prayer. And I designed ten journal-style prayer pages to apply my Passionate Prayer Growth Plan that became the foundation of this Passionate Prayer Notebook:

Prayer Journal

Scripture Prayer

Listening to God

Thank You, Lord

Quotes on Prayer

Books on Prayer

Adventure in Prayer

Knowing God

ACTS Prayer

Prayer Focus

These pages are all ways to grow in your life of prayer. In fact, each page is a spiritual growth plan in itself, simply because it will draw you closer to God. In the pages that follow, I will give instructions and examples for each of the pages of this Passionate Prayer Growth Plan. Each page is a way to draw near to God, be sensitive to Him in your life, and walk closely with Him day by day and moment by moment. This plan will encourage you to add pause and rest into the rhythm of your life, focus your attention on your intimate relationship with God, and as a result, pray about everything in your life.

PRAYER JOURNAL

The very first idea that came to my mind for my prayer growth plan was to simply write out my prayers. I use the Prayer Journal page for the purpose of expressing all that is in my heart. (See next page for an example.) I liken the act of writing prayers as writing letters to the Lord. In this way, I visualize Him reading all I have written. God will lead you as you pray. When you write your prayers, you might even view them as your own psalms to the Lord.

In fact, you may even write your prayers as poetry. You will be amazed at some of the prayers that you are led to write and pray. One I have prayed frequently has been instrumental throughout my life: *Lord, may my dreams and desires be hemmed in by the boundaries of Your plans and purposes.*

Writing out your prayers to the Lord has biblical precedence. The psalms are filled with written prayers, and David is one of the finest prayer writers in history.

> To You, O LORD, I lift up my soul.
> O my God, in You I trust,
> Do not let me be ashamed;
> Do not let my enemies exult over me…
> Make me know Your ways, O LORD;
> Teach me Your paths.
> Lead me in Your truth and teach me,
> for You are the God of my salvation;
> for You I wait all the day (Psalm 25:1-2,4-5).

Can't you just hear David's heartfelt passion for God reverberate from the pages of his written prayers? What do you write on your Prayer Journal pages? Paul says, "First of all, then, I urge that entreaties and prayers, petitions and thanksgivings, be made on behalf of all men, for kings, and for all authority, so that we may lead a tranquil and quiet life in all godliness and dignity" (1 Timothy 2:1-2). You may include entreaties (supplications)—urgent heartfelt requests based on a deep need, prayers—general requests in communion with God, petitions—intercessory requests on behalf of yourself or others, and thanksgiving—praises for blessings and benefits. You may also wish to make confessions—agreements with God about your sin (1 John 1:9). And you may write out commitments and resolves—decisions of attitudes or actions toward the Lord (Psalm 31:7).

Application:

Write a prayer to the Lord using one of the Prayer Journal pages.

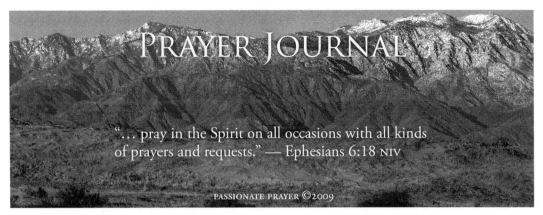

*Write your own prayers to God. Pray about everything on your heart including people, circumstances,
trials, temptations, responses to God's Word, and worship, praise, and adoration of God.*

3-25-13 - Lord, I pray that You will keep my heart soft and sensitive to You and to others. May my eyes stayed fixed on You even when I am distracted. Help me to run the race you've set before me with endurance. May You be glorified in my life no matter what I face today. As David says in Psalm 18, I love You O Lord my strength!

4-6-13 - Lord, I need strength today to keep the schedule that I have. Help me Lord in every meeting to shine for You and love others with Your love. Keep my words encouraging and help me to point others always to You.

4-10-13 - Thank You Lord for the incredible privilege to walk with You in life. You have given me everything I need. Even in the midst of my difficult circumstances, You are my strength and my refuge. I always have a place to run, as Corrie called it, a hiding place. Thank You Lord for giving me significance and purpose in life.

SCRIPTURE PRAYER

The next essential for our prayer growth plan is personalizing verses from the Bible as our own prayers to the Lord. I use a Scripture Prayer page so that the Bible becomes one of my prayer partners. (See next page for an example.) With Scripture Prayer, the object of your prayer is God and His Word, not self and the world.

John instructs us in 1 John 5:14-15 that we may be boldly confident in our prayers if we pray according to God's will: "This is the confidence which we have before Him, that, if we ask anything according to His will, He hears us. And if we know that He hears us in whatever we ask, we know that we have the requests which we have asked from Him." At a meeting of the Fellowship of Christian Athletes, Bobby Richardson, former New York Yankee second baseman, offered a prayer that is a classic in brevity and poignancy: *Dear God, Your will, nothing more, nothing less, nothing else. Amen.* We can know we are praying what is truly God's will when we pray using His Word itself. Dietrich Bonhoeffer points out that "if we wish to pray with confidence and gladness, then the words of Holy Scripture will have to be the solid basis of our prayer…The richness of the Word of God ought to determine our prayer, not the poverty of our heart."[3]

I find the psalms especially conducive to praying the Bible to the Lord. Here are two examples:

> *Lord, You are my shepherd. Because of You, I shall not want. You make me lie down in green pastures; You lead me beside quiet waters* (based on Psalm 23:1-2).

> *Lord, You are my light and my salvation; whom shall I fear? You are the defense of my life; whom shall I dread?…Lord, I want to ask You for one thing: and I seek it from You. I want to dwell in Your house all the days of my life, to behold Your beauty and to meditate in Your temple* (based on Psalm 27:1,4).

Some of my favorite prayers are paraphrases of Scripture:

Have mercy on me, a sinner (Luke 18:13).

Fill me with Your Spirit, Lord (Ephesians 5:18).

Who am I, O Lord? (1 Chronicles 29:14).

Revive me, O Lord (Psalm 119:25).

Application:

Chose a phrase, a verse, or even an entire passage from your Bible reading and write a prayer to the Lord using a Scripture Prayer page.

SCRIPTURE PRAYER

"Do not let this Book of the Law depart from your mouth; meditate on it day and night …"
— Joshua 1:8 NIV 1984

PASSIONATE PRAYER ©2009

Write your own prayers using verses & prayers in the Bible; apply the words to your life circumstances.

Bible Verse(s) ___1 Corinthians 15:58___

Lord, I pray that You will keep me steadfast, immovable, always abounding in Your work, knowing that my toil is not in vain when it is done in You.

Bible Verse(s) ___Colossians 1:9-12___

Lord, I pray that You will fill me with the knowledge of Your will in all spiritual wisdom and understanding, so that I will walk in a manner worthy of You, to please You in all respects, bearing fruit in every good work and increasing in the knowledge of You; Strengthen me with all power, according to Your glorious might, for the attaining of all steadfastness and patience. I joyously give thanks to You, who has qualified any who know You (including me) to share in the inheritance of the saints in Light.

LISTENING TO GOD

Listening to what God says in His Word is another essential in your prayer growth plan. I use a Listening to God page to emphasize the synergy between God's Word and thoughts, ideas, and actions that the Lord brings to my mind. (See next page for an example.) The writer of Hebrews tells us that "the word of God is living and active and sharper than any two-edged sword, and piercing as far as the division of soul and spirit, of both joints and marrow, and able to judge the thoughts and intentions of the heart" (Hebrews 4:12). Listen for God's voice in His Word. Silence and solitude are important starting points in your approach. Mother Teresa has said, "God is the friend of silence—we need to listen to God because it's not what we say but what He says to us and through us that matters."[4] We listen for God not in a mindless vacuum, but in the context of His Word.

The Holy Spirit knows our struggles and where we are wrestling with God's ways in our lives. I remember a time when I felt so alone that I was tearful every moment of the day. I read Psalm 45:10-11 and paraphrased it in my notebook: "Listen, daughter; the King loves your beauty." This passage is a love song about the king and his bride, and is also thought to point to the love Christ has for the church. As I read those verses on a lonely day, I was reminded of the love Christ has for me and how He sees me as beautiful. I realized how close, intimate, and ever-present my Lord always is with me, regardless of how remote I may imagine myself. In those quiet moments, listening to God, I was greatly moved and encouraged by my Lord.

Sometimes my time with God will prompt an idea to encourage someone or an idea for ministry. I like to write those ideas on my Listening to God page and then pray for God to lead and guide me in their development. I'll never forget writing out what God taught me from the four words in Genesis 8:1: "And God remembered Noah." I listened to God that day and heard Him saying to me that He surely remembers His children. It is outside the realm of His nature to ever forget us. But I needed to hear that truth, for I was feeling forgotten, left out in the cold in my prolonged trial. God spoke, and I listened. Because I wrote down what He taught me from the Word, I can look back on that written testimony of yesterday to gain new encouragement for today and abiding hope for tomorrow.

Application:

Choose a Listening to God page and write out what you hear from God in His Word and your response to Him.

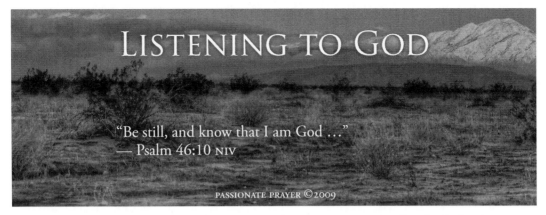

Write ideas, thoughts, and actions that come to mind during your quiet time about family, friends, ministry, prayer, quiet time, work, and encouraging others. Ask God how to act upon what you hear.

Date _____01-05-13_____

> *Idea, Thought, or Action*

This morning in my quiet time when I read Hebrews 4:12 about how the Word of God is alive and powerful, I thought about how we should always encourage others to be in the Word. Then, I thought about how to encourage my family with the Word of God. I got the idea to get a new Bible for my niece - the kind that will be easy for her to read. I'll make a quiet time basket for her to get her excited about spending time with the Lord.

> *My Response*

This is such a great idea! Why didn't I think of it before! I'll take it to her when I visit next weekend.

Date _____01-05-13_____

> *Idea, Thought, or Action*

Reading in Ruth 2:1-23 today was very powerful. I thought about how Ruth was gleaning in the fields of Boaz her kinsman redeemer. I see this as such a picture for me of living and gleaning in the fields of my Lord Jesus, who is my Redeemer. I love verse 8 where Boaz says, "Stay right here with us...don't go to any other fields." The Lord calls me to that same singlehearted, exclusive devotion to Him. I think of Psalm 37:4

> *My Response*

Lord, thank You for being my Redeemer. I love you with all my heart and soul.

THANK YOU, LORD

We need to thank the Lord in the midst of everything we face in life. What better way to enhance our prayer growth plan than using a Thank You, Lord page in our quiet time? (See next page for an example.) Paul encourages us to be "always giving thanks for all things in the name of our Lord Jesus Christ to God, even the Father" (Ephesians 5:20). This has become such a passion for me that it frequently becomes the primary focus for my prayers each day. "Ah," you say, "it's easy to thank the Lord each day when things go well. But what about when I am ill, lose my job, or become so depressed I cannot get out of bed?" For me, times of adversity and suffering have become opportunities to delve deep into the Word and express thankfulness to the Lord made possible only through the power of the Holy Spirit. Many times, I've discovered that God has plans that have not yet entered my mind. F.B. Meyer addresses this point: "Remember to give thanks 'always' for 'all' things. Whether you like the packing case or not, you may be sure that the contents are the very best that God could send you."[5] And many times, an entry of tears on my Thank You, Lord page has later become one of great joy and peace.

When Corrie and Betsie ten Boom arrived at Ravensbruck concentration camp during World War II, they discovered their barracks was swarming with fleas. Corrie cried out to Betsie, "How can we live in such a place?" Betsie began praying, "Show us how, show us how." Betsie turned to Corrie and asked her what they had read in the Bible that morning. She had read in 1 Thessalonians, "Give thanks in all circumstances; for this is God's will for you in Christ Jesus."

"That's it, Corrie! That's His answer. 'Give thanks in all circumstances!'…We can start right now to thank God for every single thing about this new barracks."

They started by thanking the Lord for the Bible they had been able to smuggle into the camp. Then Betsie prayed, "Thank You for the fleas and for…"

But Corrie interrupted, "Betsie, there's no way even God can make me grateful for a flea."

Betsie replied, "Fleas are part of this place where God has put us." Corrie and Betsie gave thanks for the fleas.

Sometime after this prayer, Betsie came to Corrie and said, "You know, we've never understood why we've had so much freedom in the big room. Well, I've found out." It was the fleas. The supervisors and guards refused to come through the door of their barrack because they wanted nothing to do with a place "crawling with fleas."[6]

Application:

Use a Thank You, Lord page to give thanks to the Lord for at least one thing today.

THANK YOU, LORD

"One of them, when he saw he was healed, came back, praising God in a loud voice. He threw himself at Jesus' feet and thanked him ..." — Luke 17:15-16 NIV

PASSIONATE PRAYER ©2009

Every day, try to write at least one thing you thank God for in your life.

Date	Lord, I am thankful for ...
3-20-13 -	the privilege of serving You Lord
3-25-13 -	the closeness of my family
3-26-13 -	my husband
3-30-13 -	being able to serve in Quiet Time Ministries
4-3-13 -	an idea for a new book
4-5-13 -	strength for today Lord
4-8-13 -	Your Word and the Holy Spirit
4-10-13 -	spending quiet time with You

QUOTES ON PRAYER

In developing my prayer growth plan, I decided I needed to read the best books on prayer and keep track of favorite quotes. Discipleship is scriptural, and I wanted to be discipled by the prayer warriors of the past and present. Paul encouraged Timothy to pass on what he had learned to others: "The things which you have heard from me in the presence of many witnesses, entrust these to faithful men who will be able to teach others also" (2 Timothy 2:2). I wanted to be one of those faithful who, with a teachable heart, could learn about prayer and then pass on what I was learning to others.

Quotable sayings are pithy and easy to remember, understand, and apply to your life. One of the quotes I memorized early on in my Christian walk was by Oswald Chambers: "Prayer does not equip us for greater works. Prayer *is* the greater work." I love that quote. But, where are you going to find good quotes on prayer? You can't go wrong with the basic staples of books, conferences, and multimedia. Once you've recorded your quotes (see example on next page), you can return to them again and again when you need encouragement to pray.

Application:

Choose some great books on prayer, then use a Quotes On Prayer page to write out your favorite quotes.

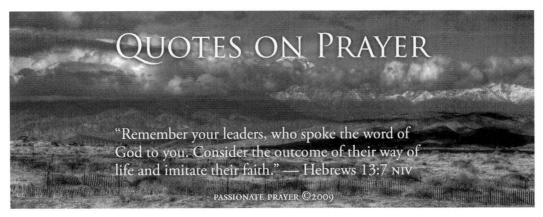

"Remember your leaders, who spoke the word of God to you. Consider the outcome of their way of life and imitate their faith." — Hebrews 13:7 NIV

PASSIONATE PRAYER ©2009

Record significant quotes and include author, source, and page numbers.

Source _____ Andrew Murray, With Christ In The School Of Prayer, p. 16 _____

Jesus never taught His disciples how to preach, only how to pray. He did not speak much of what was needed to preach well, but much of praying well. To know how to speak to God is more than knowing how to speak to man. Not power with men, but power with God is the first thing. Jesus loves to teach us how to pray.

Source _____ S.D. Gordon, Quiet Talks On Prayer, p. 15 _____

Prayer opens a whole planet to man's activities. I can as really be touching hearts for God in far away India or China through prayer, as though I were there ... his relationship is as wide as his Master's and his sympathies should be. A man may be in Africa, but if his heart be in touch with Jesus it will be burning for a world. Prayer puts us into dynamic touch with a world.

BOOKS ON PRAYER

Once I began developing my prayer growth plan, I decided I would always have a book on prayer in my quiet time basket. What makes a good book? The writer must be committed to the Lord and to the authority of God's Word. The writer should be orthodox in teaching, that is, not known to be a false or heretical teacher. Indeed, the writer of Hebrews points out that those who lead us should speak the word of God to us (Hebrews 13:7). The writer should take you directly to the Bible, with principles supported by Scripture itself. I am extremely selective in what I read. Time is short, and I'm not inclined to waste it on fluff or fancy. I want God's eternal perspective in everything I read. My favorite authors are A.W. Tozer, Andrew Murray, G. Campbell Morgan, Oswald Chambers, Amy Carmichael, Charles Spurgeon, and F.B. Meyer. I always want to know what God has taught them from the Bible.

Your interaction with the books you read will make a difference in your prayer life and the prayer lives of others. Underline favorite quotes, write comments in the margins, and copy the quotes on your Books on Prayer (see example on next page). Never underestimate the power of a quote on prayer. Remember the prayer warriors and imitate their faith.

Application:

Choose a classic book on prayer, then use a Books on Prayer page to write out your favorite quotes.

BOOKS ON PRAYER

"... godliness has value for all things ..."
— 1 Timothy 4:8 NIV

PASSIONATE PRAYER ©2009

As you read books on prayer, underlining important quotes, record page numbers with a subject–quote.

Date 01-05-13

Book Prayer   *Author* O'Hallesby

Page(s)   *Subject—Quote*

13 - the breath of the soul

14 - let Jesus into our needs

14 - to pray is to let Jesus glorify His name in the midst of our needs

17 - in the sunshine of His grace

17 - To be a Christian is in truth to have gained a place in the sun!

18 - Prayer and helplessness are inseparable. Only those who are helpless can truly pray.

21 - Prayer is for the helpless.

54 - How God answers prayer - sending the answer

59 - praying in the name of Jesus

61 - the secret prayer chamber - a resting place and also a workshop

ADVENTURE IN PRAYER

In your prayer growth plan, you will want to keep track of what God is teaching you about prayer. I have discovered the great value of chronicling my adventure with the Lord. I love using the Adventure in Prayer to write what God is teaching me (See next page for an example.) I include the date, the source, what I've learned, and my response in prayer. This is especially useful for examples of prayer throughout the Bible. Just recently, I was impressed with Abraham's persistent and bold prayer on behalf of Lot and his family. I learned from Abraham the importance of never giving up in prayer. I've learned from Hannah to pour out my soul to the Lord. I've learned from Nehemiah to pray on behalf of countries and God's covenant people. I've learned from Paul that I must always pray. We learn lessons quicker and remember them longer when we write them down.

Application:

Reflect on the last 6 months and write out what God has been teaching you about prayer on an Adventure in Prayer page. Then, once a week or even once a month, use an Adventure in Prayer page and write out the details of your adventure in prayer.

"Blessed are those whose strength is in you, whose
hearts are set on pilgrimage."
— Psalm 84:5 NIV

PASSIONATE PRAYER ©2009

*Record your journey by writing what you are learning about prayer. Include date, key scripture &
sources, and respond in prayer to God.*

Date ___01-05-13___ *Key Verse–Source* _____Philippians 4:6-7_____

What I Am Learning

The Lord does not want me to worry. Prayer is the prescription for worry. Peace
will guard my heart like a sentry keeping out all intruders that threaten to rob
me of peace.

My Response

Lord, I lay my worries and burdens at Your feet.

Date ___04-15-13___ *Key Verse–Source* _____S.D. Gordon, Quiet Talks On Prayer_____

What I Am Learning

Prayer puts me in touch with the world. The scope of God's plan includes the
world. This is powerful to me knowing that no matter what God includes me in
His plans through prayer.

My Response

Lord, I want to pray more for the world and specific countries in the world. Help
me be more faithful in this.

KNOWING GOD

Your greatest claim in life is that you know God. And nowhere is this claim more vividly expressed than in your life of prayer. God said, "Let him who boasts, boast of this, that he understands and knows Me" (Jeremiah 9:24). In Daniel 11:32 we see that "the people who know their God will display strength and take action." The Hebrew word translated "know" is *yada* and implies an actual experiential relationship with God, not an academic acquiring of facts. The more you know God, the more you will pray. The more intimate your relationship with Him, the more time you will spend with Him. E.M. Bounds said, "Those who know God the best are the richest and most powerful in prayer. Little acquaintance with God, and strangeness and coldness to Him, make prayer a rare and feeble thing."

As I developed my own prayer growth plan, I realized that every time I read the Bible in my quiet time, I learned something new about God. I decided that documenting my adventure in knowing God is another important component for prayer growth. So I devoted the Knowing God page to keep an account of all that I was learning about God. (See next page for an example.)

Whenever you study the Bible, always look for truths about who God is, what God does, and what God says.[7] You will never be disappointed in this endeavor because God reveals Himself through His Word. He spoke the Word, and by virtue of His authorship, every Word reveals His nature. Think about that for a minute. Whenever you read any book, the writing reveals the character of the author. But the Word of God is a living, God-breathed book. Paul told Timothy, "All Scripture is God-breathed and is useful for teaching, rebuking, correcting and training in righteousness, so that the man of God may be thoroughly equipped for every good work" (2 Timothy 3:16-17 NIV). Paul's words clearly show us that God is the author of the Bible. Ask Him to show Himself to you in His Word.

Application:

Reflect on the last 6 months and write out what God has been teaching you about Himself on a Knowing God page. Then, as you study God's Word in your quiet time, use a Knowing God page and write out all you are learning.

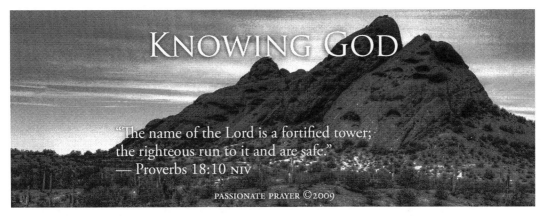

The goal in prayer, as in all of life, is to know God. As you study God's Word and pray, write what you learn when God shows you a truth about Himself.

Date _____01-05-13_____ *Key Verse–Source* _____Psalm 46:1_____

What I Am Learning

I am learning that God is my refuge and my strength. He is the One I must always run to when I need help. This is particularly important and vital in my life of prayer.

My Response

Lord, show me how to run to You as my refuge.

Date _____04-15-13_____ *Key Verse–Source* _____Genesis 1:1_____

What I Am Learning

I am learning more and more about God as Elohim, the Triune God, who created the heavens and the earth. What this means to me is that God can create something out of nothing including creating something in my impossible situations. This greatly impacts and encourages my trust in God.

My Response

Lord, thank You for creating something out of nothing and I trust You today in my impossible situation.

ACTS PRAYER

The greatest example for your life of prayer is Jesus. When you read through the Gospels—Matthew, Mark, Luke, and John—you cannot help but notice that Jesus' prayer life dominated His days and nights. He prayed before major events, He prayed for His disciples, He prayed on the way from one town to another, He prayed on the road to suffering, and He even prayed while on the cross. He shows you what to do when you face temptation—pray. He shows you what to do when popularity and success are yours—pray. He shows you what to do when you face big decisions—pray. And He shows you how to use your time wisely—pray. Luke tells us that "the news about Him was spreading even farther, and large crowds were gathering to hear Him and to be healed of their sicknesses. But Jesus Himself would often slip away to the wilderness and pray." We see in Jesus the habit of constant prayer—an ongoing conversation, walking and talking with the Father.

Jesus' life of prayer should prompt one overwhelming prayer from us just as it did from His disciples: *Lord, teach us to pray.* Jesus teaches a methodology of prayer in the Lord's Prayer (Matthew 6:9-13). This prayer is indeed Jesus' instruction on prayer, an up close and personal how-to course for His disciples. He says, "Pray, then, in this way." The Lord's prayer provides a wonderful pattern for prayer. His prayer includes worship, confession, petitions (requests), forgiveness, supplication and intercession, and praise. Sometimes I will literally pray through each phrase of the Lord's prayer and stop between each statement and amplify it with my own words of praise, worship, confession, and requests.

ACTS is a helpful acrostic incorporating elements taught in the Lord's prayer:

Adoration. I worship and praise God for who He is, what He does, and what He says.

Confession. I confess my sins to the Lord.

Thanksgiving. I thank the Lord for the blessings in my life.

Supplication. I present my requests before the Lord.

You may base your prayers on Scripture or use your own words for adoration, confession, thanksgiving, and supplication (ACTS). (See next page for examples).

Application:

In a quiet time this coming week, take some time to write out a prayer to the Lord using the ACTS Prayer page.

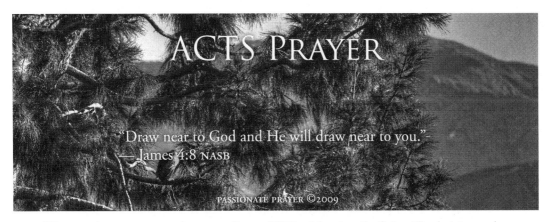

ACTS PRAYER

"Draw near to God and He will draw near to you."
—James 4:8 NASB

PASSIONATE PRAYER ©2009

Write out the prayers on your heart according to ACTS—Adoration, Confession, Thanksgiving, and Supplication. You may want to use Scripture as well as your own words.

Date ___01-05-13___

Adoration

I love you, LORD, you are my strength. You are my rock, my fortress, my protection. You are my place of safety. Psalm 18:1-2

Confession

Have mercy on me, O God, because of your unfailing love. Wash me clean purify me. Create in me a clean heart. Psalm 51

Thanksgiving

You have turned my mourning into dancing. Lord, You have clothed me with joy. I will give you thanks forever! Psalm 30:11-12

Supplication

Lord, I pray that you will deliver me and free me from all my fears. Psalm 34:4

Date ___04-15-13___

Adoration

Lord, You are faithful and compassionate and merciful. I praise You that You are the God of details who loves even me.

Confession

Lord, I confess my unbelief and my habit of worrying. Help my unbelief, dear Lord.

Thanksgiving

Lord, thank you for loving me and for guiding me, especially in these days of uncertainty in my own life.

Supplication

Lord, make me a woman of faith who believes what You say, no matter what.

PRAYER FOCUS

God is just waiting to pour out His blessings on us. It is not that God is withholding His blessing, but He pours out His blessing to His children who ask in the context of an intimate relationship with their loving Father. Just imagine your God asking you, "Child, what do you want?"

One of my favorite ways to pray is to imagine myself in God's throne room, before my Lord, who is inviting me to pray to Him. This way of praying has become such a frequent habit for me that I like to devote a Prayer Focus page for it in my quiet time. (See next page for an example.) On this page I list my top five prayer requests for special focus. I think, *If I could ask God anything, what would I ask?*

Friends, this is a very powerful way to pray, for you will often ask Him for things that may seem bold or even extraordinary. But God delights in just such prayers. You never want it to be said that you don't have because you never asked. You may ask, "Isn't that a kind of selfish or presumptuous praying?" Be encouraged; God already knows what is in your heart. You will discover that God will often lead you to change your prayers to even more extraordinary requests!

Then, as I see God answer my prayers, I record what He has done, along with the date, on the Prayer Focus page. Then I like to write out what I'm learning along with the date of my insights so that I can see how God is working through my life of passionate prayer to transform me for His glory.

Application:

Use a Prayer Focus page in one of your quiet times this week, pouring out your heart to the Lord with those things that are burdening you the most. Then return to the Prayer Focus page in the next few weeks and see how God has been answering your prayers. Then write out what you have learned.

PRAYER FOCUS

"The prayer of a righteous person is powerful and effective." — James 5:16 TNIV

PASSIONATE PRAYER ©2009

Write out your top prayers, requests,and answers to prayer for a selected period of time—every month, week, or day. You may want to use the daily focus to enhance your prayer time. Daily Focus: Sunday— church, pastors, leaders, Monday—nation, Tuesday—world, Wednesday—community, Thursday— missionaries and ministries, Friday—your ministry, Saturday—revival

My Prayers   Dates–Month, Week, Day____4/1/07_____

1. Messages on spiritual growth for upcoming SCC Women's Retreat from 2 Peter 3:18.

2. The next books I write - a book on the adventure of knowing God and one on prayer.

3. My dear mother.

4. My organization of time this next year to accomplish much in Your name, dear Lord.

5. The filming of message for Walking With The God Who Cares.

God's Answers

April 2007 - 4 messages that led to a new book on spiritual growth.

July 2008 - Lord, thank You for helping me write two books all about trusting in Your names.

Dec 2007 - Thank you Lord for guiding us.

March 2008 - Thank you Lord for giving me the discipline to do more than I thought I could do.

June 2011 Thank You Lord for a great location and Your strength.

What I'm Learning

4-1-08 - I am learning to walk and live by faith. I would say my big words over the last year have been trust, faith, and believe.

_____

HOW TO USE THE PASSIONATE PRAYER NOTEBOOK

Be anxious for nothing, but in everything by prayer and supplication with thanksgiving let your requests be made known to God. And the peace of God, which surpasses all comprehension, will guard your hearts and your minds in Christ Jesus.

PHILIPPIANS 4:6-7

Drawing near to God in prayer not only impacts your life circumstances, it also changes you. Prayer, according to Philippians 4:6-7, is the solution for anxiety and worry, and brings peace to your heart. Imagine being able to walk in rest and peace in spite of turbulent circumstances. Prayer will help you stand strong in the midst of many storms as you stay close to your Lord in constant communication.

The Passionate Prayer Notebook, with ten different prayer pages, will help you grow deeper in your life of passionate prayer. So, where do you begin? The best way is to familiarize yourself with each of the ten pages along with the instructions in Chapter 3. Then, I encourage you to use one of each of the ten pages you will find in the next section of this notebook. You might begin with the Prayer Journal page and write a prayer to the Lord, as though you were writing Him a letter. Choose a favorite passage of Scripture, and personalize it by writing a prayer to the Lord on the Scripture Prayer page. As you experiment with the different prayer pages, you may wonder if you are "doing it right." I felt the same way when I first began my prayer growth plan using these different prayer pages. Let me just release you from that idea and encourage you to experiment with all the different pages. Ask the Lord to teach you and guide you as you draw near to Him in prayer. Be sure to have your Bible with you at all times because God will speak to you in His Word. You will begin to sense that He is the One leading you on this great adventure. After all, there is no one who longs for you to be passionate about prayer more than the Lord Himself. He desires your company. He wants you to know Him and longs for an intimate relationship with you. With time and practice, these pages will become a great tool to help you grow in prayer. You will have favorites that you will enjoy the most. But always remember, the best way to learn to pray is to pray.

So how does *The Passionate Prayer Notebook* work with your quiet time? Keep it close by as a resource along with all your other quiet time materials including your Bible, devotionals, and Bible studies. I encourage you to always be reading through a book on prayer in your quiet time. You can use the Quotes on Prayer and Books on Prayer pages for your reading on prayer. Then, in response to your time in God's Word, take some time to Adore God in Prayer, the third essential in The P.R.A.Y.E.R. Quiet Time Plan. Try using the different prayer pages to go deeper in prayer, such as the Prayer Journal, Scripture Prayers, Listening to God, Thank You, Lord, ACTS Prayer, and/or Prayer Focus. Then, from time to time, use the Adventure in Prayer and Knowing God pages to write out what God is teaching you about prayer and your relationship with Him.

And so now, the adventure really begins. As you begin your adventure in passionate prayer, I invite you to take time alone with the Lord in the quiet time that follows, "The Privilege of Prayer." And then, know that passionate prayer is an adventure of learning and growing throughout your life. Prayer is an experience that grows deeper and more precious with time. The more you know your Lord, the more you will pray. And the more you pray, the more you will know your Lord. So, dear friend, whether you are a seasoned traveler with the Lord or have just begun the journey, I want to pray for your time with Him in prayer.

MY PRAYER FOR YOU

Lord Jesus, I pray for this one who desires to know You more and grow in their life of prayer with you. They have The Passionate Prayer Notebook and are ready to embark on a new adventure with you in prayer. I ask that You will be their Teacher, and draw them close to Your heart. Will you give them a deeper passion for prayer through the power of the Holy Spirit. Teach them powerful truths in Your Word and lead them to great books on prayer. Transform their hearts, more and more with each passing day, making them the person You want them to be. May they glorify You, and may they walk wholeheartedly with You every day of their life on earth. And may they someday hear those wonderful words from You when they see You face to face: "Well done, good and faithful servant." In Jesus' Name, Amen. — Catherine Martin

THE PRIVILEGE OF PRAYER

Devote yourselves to prayer.
COLOSSIANS 4:2

PREPARE YOUR HEART

One of the greatest privileges you've been given is the high privilege of prayer—walking and talking with God Himself. You've seen this week that the Bible has much to say about prayer. As you draw near to God in quiet time, you are going to look firsthand at some of those important verses and learn about prayer. Turn to God now and ask Him to quiet your heart and speak to you in His Word.

READ AND STUDY GOD'S WORD

1. In the Sermon on the Mount, Jesus taught His audience about God's perspective of prayer and what prayer really means. Read the following passages of Scripture and write what you learn about prayer:

Matthew 6:5-15

Matthew 7:7-12

2. Read the following verses on prayer and underline those words and phrases that mean the most to you:

"If you abide in Me, and My words abide in you, ask whatever you wish, and it will be done for you" (John 15:7).

"Be anxious for nothing, but in everything by prayer and supplication with thanksgiving let your requests be made known to God. And the peace of God, which surpasses all comprehension, will guard your hearts and your minds in Christ Jesus" (Philippians 4:6-7).

"Devote yourselves to prayer, keeping alert in it with an attitude of thanksgiving" (Colossians 4:2).

"First of all, then, I urge that entreaties and prayers, petitions and thanksgivings, be made on behalf of all men" (1 Timothy 2:1).

"Therefore, confess your sins to one another, and pray for one another so that you may be healed. The effective prayer of a righteous man can accomplish much" (James 5:16).

"For the eyes of the Lord are toward the righteous. And His ears attend to their prayer" (1 Peter 3:12).

ADORE GOD IN PRAYER

Talk with the Lord today about your desire to learn all about prayer and grow in your life of prayer.

YIELD YOURSELF TO GOD

Prayer is a daring venture into speech that juxtaposes our words with the sharply alive words that pierce and divide souls and spirit, joints and marrow, pitilessly exposing every thought and intention of the heart (Hebrews 4:12-13; Revelation 1:16). If we had kept our mouths shut we would not have involved ourselves in such a relentlessly fearsome exposure…Praying puts us at risk of getting involved in God's conditions…Praying most often doesn't get us what we want but what God wants, something quite at variance with what we conceive to be in our best interests.[1]

EUGENE PETERSON

Prayer is something deeper than words. It is present in the soul before it has been formulated in words. And it abides in the soul after the last words of prayer have passed over our lips. Prayer is an attitude of our hearts, an attitude of mind. Prayer is a definite attitude of our hearts toward God, an attitude which He in heaven immediately recognizes as prayer, as an appeal to His heart. Whether it takes the form of words or not, does not mean anything to God, only to ourselves.[2]

OLE HALLESBY

ENJOY HIS PRESENCE

How would you define prayer? What have you learned about prayer this week that will help you walk and talk with God more?

REST IN HIS LOVE

"Ask, and it will be given to you; seek, and you will find; knock, and it will be opened to you. For everyone who asks receives, and he who seeks finds, and to him who knocks it will be opened" (Matthew 7:7-8).

THE PASSIONATE PRAYER
NOTEBOOK PAGES

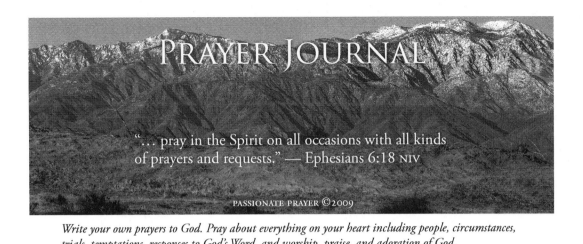

PRAYER JOURNAL

"… pray in the Spirit on all occasions with all kinds of prayers and requests." — Ephesians 6:18 NIV

PASSIONATE PRAYER ©2009

Write your own prayers to God. Pray about everything on your heart including people, circumstances, trials, temptations, responses to God's Word, and worship, praise, and adoration of God.

PRAYER JOURNAL

"… pray in the Spirit on all occasions with all kinds of prayers and requests." — Ephesians 6:18 NIV

Write your own prayers to God. Pray about everything on your heart including people, circumstances, trials, temptations, responses to God's Word, and worship, praise, and adoration of God.

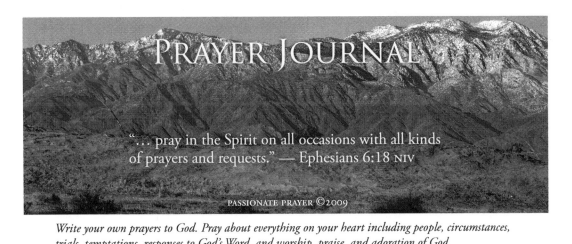

Prayer Journal

"… pray in the Spirit on all occasions with all kinds of prayers and requests." — Ephesians 6:18 NIV

Write your own prayers to God. Pray about everything on your heart including people, circumstances, trials, temptations, responses to God's Word, and worship, praise, and adoration of God.

PRAYER JOURNAL

"... pray in the Spirit on all occasions with all kinds of prayers and requests." — Ephesians 6:18 NIV

Write your own prayers to God. Pray about everything on your heart including people, circumstances, trials, temptations, responses to God's Word, and worship, praise, and adoration of God.

PRAYER JOURNAL

"... pray in the Spirit on all occasions with all kinds
of prayers and requests." — Ephesians 6:18 NIV

PASSIONATE PRAYER ©2009

*Write your own prayers to God. Pray about everything on your heart including people, circumstances,
trials, temptations, responses to God's Word, and worship, praise, and adoration of God.*

PRAYER JOURNAL

"… pray in the Spirit on all occasions with all kinds of prayers and requests." — Ephesians 6:18 NIV

Write your own prayers to God. Pray about everything on your heart including people, circumstances, trials, temptations, responses to God's Word, and worship, praise, and adoration of God.

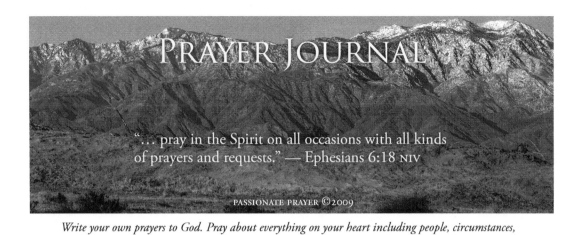

PRAYER JOURNAL

"... pray in the Spirit on all occasions with all kinds
of prayers and requests." — Ephesians 6:18 NIV

PASSIONATE PRAYER ©2009

Write your own prayers to God. Pray about everything on your heart including people, circumstances, trials, temptations, responses to God's Word, and worship, praise, and adoration of God.

PRAYER JOURNAL

"... pray in the Spirit on all occasions with all kinds of prayers and requests." — Ephesians 6:18 NIV

Write your own prayers to God. Pray about everything on your heart including people, circumstances, trials, temptations, responses to God's Word, and worship, praise, and adoration of God.

PRAYER JOURNAL

"... pray in the Spirit on all occasions with all kinds of prayers and requests." — Ephesians 6:18 NIV

Write your own prayers to God. Pray about everything on your heart including people, circumstances, trials, temptations, responses to God's Word, and worship, praise, and adoration of God.

PRAYER JOURNAL

"... pray in the Spirit on all occasions with all kinds of prayers and requests." — Ephesians 6:18 NIV

Write your own prayers to God. Pray about everything on your heart including people, circumstances, trials, temptations, responses to God's Word, and worship, praise, and adoration of God.

PRAYER JOURNAL

"… pray in the Spirit on all occasions with all kinds
of prayers and requests." — Ephesians 6:18 NIV

Write your own prayers to God. Pray about everything on your heart including people, circumstances, trials, temptations, responses to God's Word, and worship, praise, and adoration of God.

PRAYER JOURNAL

"... pray in the Spirit on all occasions with all kinds of prayers and requests." — Ephesians 6:18 NIV

Write your own prayers to God. Pray about everything on your heart including people, circumstances, trials, temptations, responses to God's Word, and worship, praise, and adoration of God.

PRAYER JOURNAL

"... pray in the Spirit on all occasions with all kinds of prayers and requests." — Ephesians 6:18 NIV

PASSIONATE PRAYER ©2009

Write your own prayers to God. Pray about everything on your heart including people, circumstances, trials, temptations, responses to God's Word, and worship, praise, and adoration of God.

PRAYER JOURNAL

"… pray in the Spirit on all occasions with all kinds of prayers and requests." — Ephesians 6:18 NIV

PASSIONATE PRAYER ©2009

Write your own prayers to God. Pray about everything on your heart including people, circumstances, trials, temptations, responses to God's Word, and worship, praise, and adoration of God.

PRAYER JOURNAL

"… pray in the Spirit on all occasions with all kinds of prayers and requests." — Ephesians 6:18 NIV

PASSIONATE PRAYER ©2009

Write your own prayers to God. Pray about everything on your heart including people, circumstances, trials, temptations, responses to God's Word, and worship, praise, and adoration of God.

PRAYER JOURNAL

"... pray in the Spirit on all occasions with all kinds of prayers and requests." — Ephesians 6:18 NIV

Write your own prayers to God. Pray about everything on your heart including people, circumstances, trials, temptations, responses to God's Word, and worship, praise, and adoration of God.

PRAYER JOURNAL

"... pray in the Spirit on all occasions with all kinds of prayers and requests." — Ephesians 6:18 NIV

Write your own prayers to God. Pray about everything on your heart including people, circumstances, trials, temptations, responses to God's Word, and worship, praise, and adoration of God.

PRAYER JOURNAL

"… pray in the Spirit on all occasions with all kinds of prayers and requests." — Ephesians 6:18 NIV

Write your own prayers to God. Pray about everything on your heart including people, circumstances, trials, temptations, responses to God's Word, and worship, praise, and adoration of God.

PRAYER JOURNAL

"… pray in the Spirit on all occasions with all kinds of prayers and requests." — Ephesians 6:18 NIV

PASSIONATE PRAYER ©2009

Write your own prayers to God. Pray about everything on your heart including people, circumstances, trials, temptations, responses to God's Word, and worship, praise, and adoration of God.

PRAYER JOURNAL

"… pray in the Spirit on all occasions with all kinds of prayers and requests." — Ephesians 6:18 NIV

Write your own prayers to God. Pray about everything on your heart including people, circumstances, trials, temptations, responses to God's Word, and worship, praise, and adoration of God.

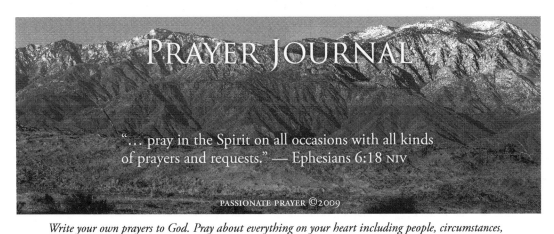

PRAYER JOURNAL

"... pray in the Spirit on all occasions with all kinds of prayers and requests." — Ephesians 6:18 NIV

PASSIONATE PRAYER ©2009

Write your own prayers to God. Pray about everything on your heart including people, circumstances, trials, temptations, responses to God's Word, and worship, praise, and adoration of God.

PRAYER JOURNAL

"... pray in the Spirit on all occasions with all kinds of prayers and requests." — Ephesians 6:18 NIV

Write your own prayers to God. Pray about everything on your heart including people, circumstances, trials, temptations, responses to God's Word, and worship, praise, and adoration of God.

PRAYER JOURNAL

"... pray in the Spirit on all occasions with all kinds of prayers and requests." — Ephesians 6:18 NIV

PASSIONATE PRAYER ©2009

Write your own prayers to God. Pray about everything on your heart including people, circumstances, trials, temptations, responses to God's Word, and worship, praise, and adoration of God.

PRAYER JOURNAL

"... pray in the Spirit on all occasions with all kinds of prayers and requests." — Ephesians 6:18 NIV

Write your own prayers to God. Pray about everything on your heart including people, circumstances, trials, temptations, responses to God's Word, and worship, praise, and adoration of God.

Prayer Journal

Write your own prayers to God. Pray about everything on your heart including people, circumstances, trials, temptations, responses to God's Word, and worship, praise, and adoration of God.

Prayer Journal

"... pray in the Spirit on all occasions with all kinds of prayers and requests." — Ephesians 6:18 NIV

Write your own prayers to God. Pray about everything on your heart including people, circumstances, trials, temptations, responses to God's Word, and worship, praise, and adoration of God.

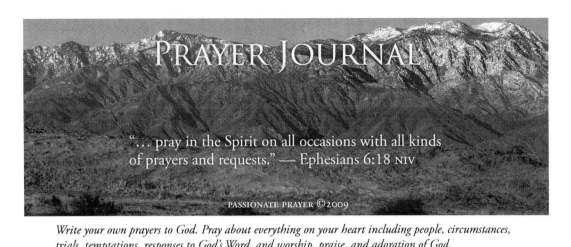

Prayer Journal

"... pray in the Spirit on all occasions with all kinds of prayers and requests." — Ephesians 6:18 NIV

PASSIONATE PRAYER ©2009

Write your own prayers to God. Pray about everything on your heart including people, circumstances, trials, temptations, responses to God's Word, and worship, praise, and adoration of God.

PRAYER JOURNAL

"... pray in the Spirit on all occasions with all kinds
of prayers and requests." — Ephesians 6:18 NIV

Write your own prayers to God. Pray about everything on your heart including people, circumstances, trials, temptations, responses to God's Word, and worship, praise, and adoration of God.

Prayer Journal

"... pray in the Spirit on all occasions with all kinds
of prayers and requests." — Ephesians 6:18 NIV

Write your own prayers to God. Pray about everything on your heart including people, circumstances, trials, temptations, responses to God's Word, and worship, praise, and adoration of God.

Prayer Journal

"... pray in the Spirit on all occasions with all kinds of prayers and requests." — Ephesians 6:18 NIV

Write your own prayers to God. Pray about everything on your heart including people, circumstances, trials, temptations, responses to God's Word, and worship, praise, and adoration of God.

SCRIPTURE PRAYER

"Do not let this Book of the Law depart from your mouth; meditate on it day and night ..."
— Joshua 1:8 NIV 1984

PASSIONATE PRAYER ©2009

Write your own prayers using verses & prayers in the Bible; apply the words to your life circumstances.

Bible Verse(s) _____

_____
_____
_____
_____
_____
_____
_____
_____
_____
_____

Bible Verse(s) _____

_____
_____
_____
_____
_____
_____
_____
_____
_____
_____
_____

SCRIPTURE PRAYER

"Do not let this Book of the Law depart from your mouth; meditate on it day and night ..."
— Joshua 1:8 NIV 1984

Write your own prayers using verses & prayers in the Bible; apply the words to your life circumstances.

Bible Verse(s) _____

....
....
....
....
....
....
....
....
....
....

Bible Verse(s) _____

....
....
....
....
....
....
....
....
....
....

SCRIPTURE PRAYER

"Do not let this Book of the Law depart from your mouth; meditate on it day and night ..."
— Joshua 1:8 NIV 1984

PASSIONATE PRAYER ©2009

Write your own prayers using verses & prayers in the Bible; apply the words to your life circumstances.

Bible Verse(s) _____

Bible Verse(s) _____

SCRIPTURE PRAYER

"Do not let this Book of the Law depart from your
mouth; meditate on it day and night ..."
— Joshua 1:8 NIV 1984

Write your own prayers using verses & prayers in the Bible; apply the words to your life circumstances.

Bible Verse(s) _____

....

....

....

....

....

....

....

....

Bible Verse(s) _____

....

....

....

....

....

....

....

....

SCRIPTURE PRAYER

"Do not let this Book of the Law depart from your
mouth; meditate on it day and night …"
— Joshua 1:8 NIV 1984

Write your own prayers using verses & prayers in the Bible; apply the words to your life circumstances.

Bible Verse(s) _____

_____

_____

_____

_____

_____

_____

_____

_____

_____

_____

Bible Verse(s) _____

_____

_____

_____

_____

_____

_____

_____

_____

_____

_____

_____

SCRIPTURE PRAYER

"Do not let this Book of the Law depart from your mouth; meditate on it day and night …"
— Joshua 1:8 NIV 1984

PASSIONATE PRAYER ©2009

Write your own prayers using verses & prayers in the Bible; apply the words to your life circumstances.

Bible Verse(s) _____

....

....

....

....

....

....

....

....

Bible Verse(s) _____

....

....

....

....

....

....

....

....

SCRIPTURE PRAYER

"Do not let this Book of the Law depart from your mouth; meditate on it day and night …"
— Joshua 1:8 NIV 1984

PASSIONATE PRAYER ©2009

Write your own prayers using verses & prayers in the Bible; apply the words to your life circumstances.

Bible Verse(s) _____

....

....

....

....

....

....

....

....

Bible Verse(s) _____

....

....

....

....

....

....

....

....

SCRIPTURE PRAYER

"Do not let this Book of the Law depart from your
mouth; meditate on it day and night ..."
— Joshua 1:8 NIV 1984

PASSIONATE PRAYER ©2009

Write your own prayers using verses & prayers in the Bible; apply the words to your life circumstances.

Bible Verse(s) _____

_____

_____

_____

_____

_____

_____

_____

_____

_____

Bible Verse(s) _____

_____

_____

_____

_____

_____

_____

_____

_____

SCRIPTURE PRAYER

"Do not let this Book of the Law depart from your mouth; meditate on it day and night …"
— Joshua 1:8 NIV 1984

PASSIONATE PRAYER ©2009

Write your own prayers using verses & prayers in the Bible; apply the words to your life circumstances.

Bible Verse(s) _____

....
....
....
....
....
....
....
....
....
....

Bible Verse(s) _____

....
....
....
....
....
....
....
....
....
....

SCRIPTURE PRAYER

"Do not let this Book of the Law depart from your mouth; meditate on it day and night …"
— Joshua 1:8 NIV 1984

PASSIONATE PRAYER ©2009

Write your own prayers using verses & prayers in the Bible; apply the words to your life circumstances.

Bible Verse(s) _____

....
....
....
....
....
....
....
....

Bible Verse(s) _____

....
....
....
....
....
....
....
....

SCRIPTURE PRAYER

"Do not let this Book of the Law depart from your
mouth; meditate on it day and night …"
— Joshua 1:8 NIV 1984

Write your own prayers using verses & prayers in the Bible; apply the words to your life circumstances.

Bible Verse(s) _____

_____

_____

_____

_____

_____

_____

_____

_____

_____

Bible Verse(s) _____

_____

_____

_____

_____

_____

_____

_____

_____

_____

SCRIPTURE PRAYER

"Do not let this Book of the Law depart from your mouth; meditate on it day and night …"
— Joshua 1:8 NIV 1984

PASSIONATE PRAYER ©2009

Write your own prayers using verses & prayers in the Bible; apply the words to your life circumstances.

Bible Verse(s) _____

_____
_____
_____
_____
_____
_____
_____
_____
_____

Bible Verse(s) _____

_____
_____
_____
_____
_____
_____
_____
_____
_____

SCRIPTURE PRAYER

"Do not let this Book of the Law depart from your
mouth; meditate on it day and night …"
— Joshua 1:8 NIV 1984

Write your own prayers using verses & prayers in the Bible; apply the words to your life circumstances.

Bible Verse(s) _____

_____

_____

_____

_____

_____

_____

_____

_____

_____

_____

Bible Verse(s) _____

_____

_____

_____

_____

_____

_____

_____

_____

_____

_____

_____

SCRIPTURE PRAYER

"Do not let this Book of the Law depart from your mouth; meditate on it day and night …"
— Joshua 1:8 NIV 1984

PASSIONATE PRAYER ©2009

Write your own prayers using verses & prayers in the Bible; apply the words to your life circumstances.

Bible Verse(s) _____

....

....

....

....

....

....

....

....

....

....

Bible Verse(s) _____

....

....

....

....

....

....

....

....

....

....

....

SCRIPTURE PRAYER

"Do not let this Book of the Law depart from your mouth; meditate on it day and night ..."
— Joshua 1:8 NIV 1984

PASSIONATE PRAYER ©2009

Write your own prayers using verses & prayers in the Bible; apply the words to your life circumstances.

Bible Verse(s) _____

_____
_____
_____
_____
_____
_____
_____
_____
_____

Bible Verse(s) _____

_____
_____
_____
_____
_____
_____
_____
_____
_____
_____

SCRIPTURE PRAYER

"Do not let this Book of the Law depart from your mouth; meditate on it day and night ..."
— Joshua 1:8 NIV 1984

Write your own prayers using verses & prayers in the Bible; apply the words to your life circumstances.

Bible Verse(s) _____

_____

_____

_____

_____

_____

_____

_____

_____

_____

_____

Bible Verse(s) _____

_____

_____

_____

_____

_____

_____

_____

_____

_____

_____

SCRIPTURE PRAYER

"Do not let this Book of the Law depart from your mouth; meditate on it day and night …"
— Joshua 1:8 NIV 1984

PASSIONATE PRAYER ©2009

Write your own prayers using verses & prayers in the Bible; apply the words to your life circumstances.

Bible Verse(s) _____

_____

_____

_____

_____

_____

_____

_____

_____

Bible Verse(s) _____

_____

_____

_____

_____

_____

_____

_____

_____

Scripture Prayer

> "Do not let this Book of the Law depart from your mouth; meditate on it day and night …"
> — Joshua 1:8 NIV 1984

Write your own prayers using verses & prayers in the Bible; apply the words to your life circumstances.

Bible Verse(s) _____

....

....

....

....

....

....

....

....

....

Bible Verse(s) _____

....

....

....

....

....

....

....

....

....

SCRIPTURE PRAYER

"Do not let this Book of the Law depart from your mouth; meditate on it day and night ..."
— Joshua 1:8 NIV 1984

Write your own prayers using verses & prayers in the Bible; apply the words to your life circumstances.

Bible Verse(s) _____

_____

_____

_____

_____

_____

_____

_____

_____

Bible Verse(s) _____

_____

_____

_____

_____

_____

_____

_____

_____

_____

SCRIPTURE PRAYER

"Do not let this Book of the Law depart from your
mouth; meditate on it day and night ..."
— Joshua 1:8 NIV 1984

Write your own prayers using verses & prayers in the Bible; apply the words to your life circumstances.

Bible Verse(s) _____

....

....

....

....

....

....

....

....

....

Bible Verse(s) _____

....

....

....

....

....

....

....

....

....

SCRIPTURE PRAYER

"Do not let this Book of the Law depart from your mouth; meditate on it day and night ..."
— Joshua 1:8 NIV 1984

PASSIONATE PRAYER ©2009

Write your own prayers using verses & prayers in the Bible; apply the words to your life circumstances.

Bible Verse(s) _____

....
....
....
....
....
....
....
....
....

Bible Verse(s) _____

....
....
....
....
....
....
....
....
....

SCRIPTURE PRAYER

"Do not let this Book of the Law depart from your mouth; meditate on it day and night …"
— Joshua 1:8 NIV 1984

PASSIONATE PRAYER ©2009

Write your own prayers using verses & prayers in the Bible; apply the words to your life circumstances.

Bible Verse(s) _____

....
....
....
....
....
....
....
....
....

Bible Verse(s) _____

....
....
....
....
....
....
....
....
....

SCRIPTURE PRAYER

"Do not let this Book of the Law depart from your mouth; meditate on it day and night …"
— Joshua 1:8 NIV 1984

PASSIONATE PRAYER ©2009

Write your own prayers using verses & prayers in the Bible; apply the words to your life circumstances.

Bible Verse(s) _____

_____
_____
_____
_____
_____
_____
_____
_____
_____
_____

Bible Verse(s) _____

_____
_____
_____
_____
_____
_____
_____
_____
_____
_____

SCRIPTURE PRAYER

"Do not let this Book of the Law depart from your
mouth; meditate on it day and night ..."
— Joshua 1:8 NIV 1984

PASSIONATE PRAYER ©2009

Write your own prayers using verses & prayers in the Bible; apply the words to your life circumstances.

Bible Verse(s) _____

....
....
....
....
....
....
....
....
....

Bible Verse(s) _____

....
....
....
....
....
....
....
....
....
....
....

SCRIPTURE PRAYER

"Do not let this Book of the Law depart from your
mouth; meditate on it day and night …"
— Joshua 1:8 NIV 1984

Write your own prayers using verses & prayers in the Bible; apply the words to your life circumstances.

Bible Verse(s) _____

. . . .

. . . .

. . . .

. . . .

. . . .

. . . .

. . . .

. . . .

Bible Verse(s) _____

. . . .

. . . .

. . . .

. . . .

. . . .

. . . .

. . . .

. . . .

SCRIPTURE PRAYER

"Do not let this Book of the Law depart from your
mouth; meditate on it day and night ..."
— Joshua 1:8 NIV 1984

Write your own prayers using verses & prayers in the Bible; apply the words to your life circumstances.

Bible Verse(s) _____

....

....

....

....

....

....

....

....

....

Bible Verse(s) _____

....

....

....

....

....

....

....

....

....

SCRIPTURE PRAYER

"Do not let this Book of the Law depart from your mouth; meditate on it day and night …"
— Joshua 1:8 NIV 1984

PASSIONATE PRAYER ©2009

Write your own prayers using verses & prayers in the Bible; apply the words to your life circumstances.

Bible Verse(s) _____

_____

_____

_____

_____

_____

_____

_____

_____

_____

Bible Verse(s) _____

_____

_____

_____

_____

_____

_____

_____

_____

_____

SCRIPTURE PRAYER

"Do not let this Book of the Law depart from your
mouth; meditate on it day and night ..."
— Joshua 1:8 NIV 1984

Write your own prayers using verses & prayers in the Bible; apply the words to your life circumstances.

Bible Verse(s) _____

....

....

....

....

....

....

....

....

....

....

Bible Verse(s) _____

....

....

....

....

....

....

....

....

....

....

SCRIPTURE PRAYER

"Do not let this Book of the Law depart from your mouth; meditate on it day and night …"
— Joshua 1:8 NIV 1984

PASSIONATE PRAYER ©2009

Write your own prayers using verses & prayers in the Bible; apply the words to your life circumstances.

Bible Verse(s) _____

....

....

....

....

....

....

....

....

....

....

Bible Verse(s) _____

....

....

....

....

....

....

....

....

....

....

SCRIPTURE PRAYER

"Do not let this Book of the Law depart from your mouth; meditate on it day and night ..."
— Joshua 1:8 NIV 1984

PASSIONATE PRAYER ©2009

Write your own prayers using verses & prayers in the Bible; apply the words to your life circumstances.

Bible Verse(s) _____

....

....

....

....

....

....

....

....

....

Bible Verse(s) _____

....

....

....

....

....

....

....

....

....

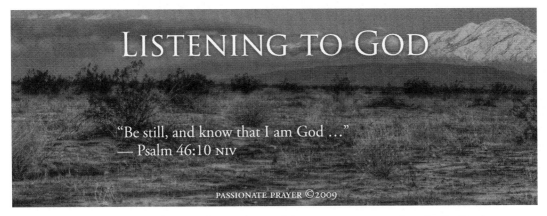

LISTENING TO GOD

"Be still, and know that I am God ..."
— Psalm 46:10 NIV

PASSIONATE PRAYER ©2009

Write ideas, thoughts, and actions that come to mind during your quiet time about family, friends, ministry, prayer, quiet time, work, and encouraging others. Ask God how to act upon what you hear.

Date _____

Idea, Thought, or Action

My Response

Date _____

Idea, Thought, or Action

My Response

LISTENING TO GOD

"Be still, and know that I am God …"
— Psalm 46:10 NIV

PASSIONATE PRAYER ©2009

Write ideas, thoughts, and actions that come to mind during your quiet time about family, friends, ministry, prayer, quiet time, work, and encouraging others. Ask God how to act upon what you hear.

Date _____

Idea, Thought, or Action

My Response

Date _____

Idea, Thought, or Action

My Response

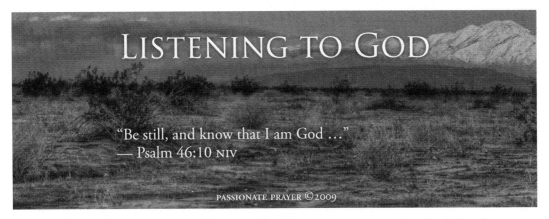

LISTENING TO GOD

"Be still, and know that I am God ..."
— Psalm 46:10 NIV

PASSIONATE PRAYER ©2009

Write ideas, thoughts, and actions that come to mind during your quiet time about family, friends, ministry, prayer, quiet time, work, and encouraging others. Ask God how to act upon what you hear.

Date _____

Idea, Thought, or Action

My Response

Date _____

Idea, Thought, or Action

My Response

LISTENING TO GOD

"Be still, and know that I am God ..."
— Psalm 46:10 NIV

PASSIONATE PRAYER ©2009

Write ideas, thoughts, and actions that come to mind during your quiet time about family, friends, ministry, prayer, quiet time, work, and encouraging others. Ask God how to act upon what you hear.

Date _____

Idea, Thought, or Action

My Response

Date _____

Idea, Thought, or Action

My Response

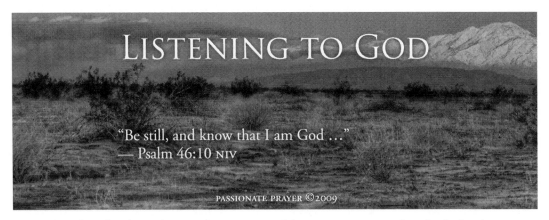

LISTENING TO GOD

"Be still, and know that I am God ..."
— Psalm 46:10 NIV

PASSIONATE PRAYER ©2009

Write ideas, thoughts, and actions that come to mind during your quiet time about family, friends, ministry, prayer, quiet time, work, and encouraging others. Ask God how to act upon what you hear.

Date _____

Idea, Thought, or Action

My Response

Date _____

Idea, Thought, or Action

My Response

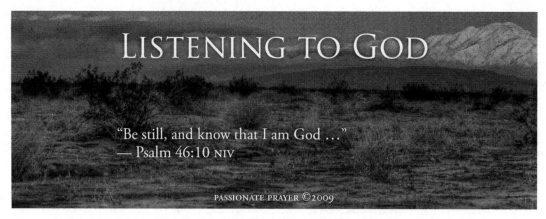

LISTENING TO GOD

"Be still, and know that I am God …"
— Psalm 46:10 NIV

PASSIONATE PRAYER ©2009

Write ideas, thoughts, and actions that come to mind during your quiet time about family, friends, ministry, prayer, quiet time, work, and encouraging others. Ask God how to act upon what you hear.

Date _____

Idea, Thought, or Action

My Response

Date _____

Idea, Thought, or Action

My Response

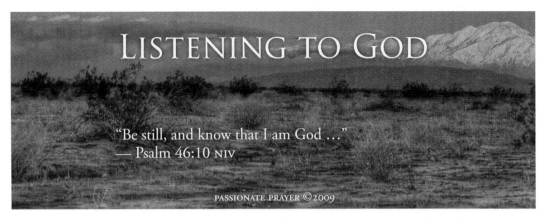

LISTENING TO GOD

"Be still, and know that I am God …"
— Psalm 46:10 NIV

PASSIONATE PRAYER ©2009

Write ideas, thoughts, and actions that come to mind during your quiet time about family, friends, ministry, prayer, quiet time, work, and encouraging others. Ask God how to act upon what you hear.

Date _____

Idea, Thought, or Action

My Response

Date _____

Idea, Thought, or Action

My Response

LISTENING TO GOD

"Be still, and know that I am God ..."
— Psalm 46:10 NIV

PASSIONATE PRAYER ©2009

Write ideas, thoughts, and actions that come to mind during your quiet time about family, friends, ministry, prayer, quiet time, work, and encouraging others. Ask God how to act upon what you hear.

Date _____

Idea, Thought, or Action

My Response

Date _____

Idea, Thought, or Action

My Response

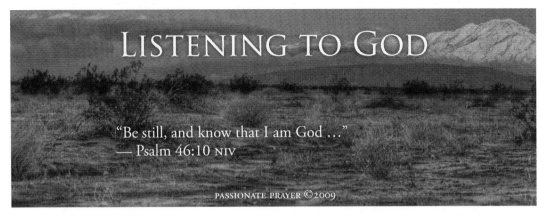

LISTENING TO GOD

"Be still, and know that I am God ..."
— Psalm 46:10 NIV

PASSIONATE PRAYER ©2009

Write ideas, thoughts, and actions that come to mind during your quiet time about family, friends, ministry, prayer, quiet time, work, and encouraging others. Ask God how to act upon what you hear.

Date _____

Idea, Thought, or Action

My Response

Date _____

Idea, Thought, or Action

My Response

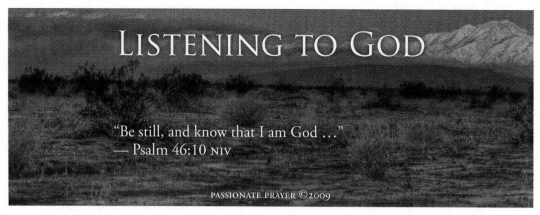

LISTENING TO GOD

"Be still, and know that I am God ..."
— Psalm 46:10 NIV

PASSIONATE PRAYER ©2009

Write ideas, thoughts, and actions that come to mind during your quiet time about family, friends, ministry, prayer, quiet time, work, and encouraging others. Ask God how to act upon what you hear.

Date _____

Idea, Thought, or Action

My Response

Date _____

Idea, Thought, or Action

My Response

LISTENING TO GOD

"Be still, and know that I am God ..."
— Psalm 46:10 NIV

PASSIONATE PRAYER ©2009

Write ideas, thoughts, and actions that come to mind during your quiet time about family, friends, ministry, prayer, quiet time, work, and encouraging others. Ask God how to act upon what you hear.

Date _____

Idea, Thought, or Action

My Response

Date _____

Idea, Thought, or Action

My Response

LISTENING TO GOD

"Be still, and know that I am God ..."
— Psalm 46:10 NIV

Write ideas, thoughts, and actions that come to mind during your quiet time about family, friends, ministry, prayer, quiet time, work, and encouraging others. Ask God how to act upon what you hear.

Date _____

Idea, Thought, or Action

My Response

Date _____

Idea, Thought, or Action

My Response

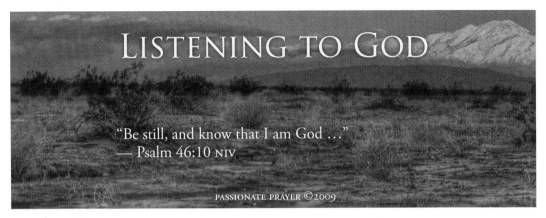

LISTENING TO GOD

"Be still, and know that I am God ..."
— Psalm 46:10 NIV

PASSIONATE PRAYER ©2009

Write ideas, thoughts, and actions that come to mind during your quiet time about family, friends, ministry, prayer, quiet time, work, and encouraging others. Ask God how to act upon what you hear.

Date _____

    Idea, Thought, or Action

    My Response

Date _____

    Idea, Thought, or Action

    My Response

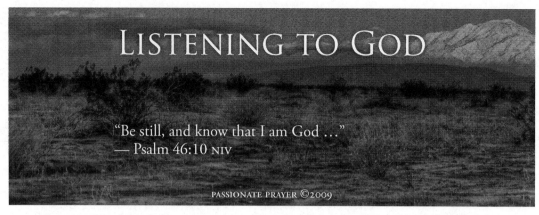

LISTENING TO GOD

"Be still, and know that I am God ..."
— Psalm 46:10 NIV

Write ideas, thoughts, and actions that come to mind during your quiet time about family, friends, ministry, prayer, quiet time, work, and encouraging others. Ask God how to act upon what you hear.

Date _____

Idea, Thought, or Action

My Response

Date _____

Idea, Thought, or Action

My Response

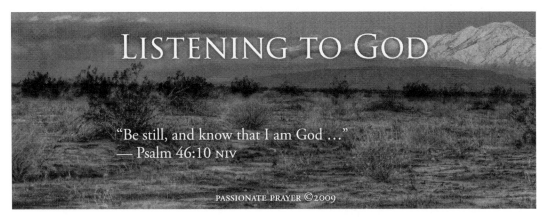

LISTENING TO GOD

"Be still, and know that I am God ..."
— Psalm 46:10 NIV

PASSIONATE PRAYER ©2009

Write ideas, thoughts, and actions that come to mind during your quiet time about family, friends, ministry, prayer, quiet time, work, and encouraging others. Ask God how to act upon what you hear.

Date _____

Idea, Thought, or Action

My Response

Date _____

Idea, Thought, or Action

My Response

LISTENING TO GOD

"Be still, and know that I am God …"
— Psalm 46:10 NIV

Write ideas, thoughts, and actions that come to mind during your quiet time about family, friends, ministry, prayer, quiet time, work, and encouraging others. Ask God how to act upon what you hear.

Date _____

Idea, Thought, or Action

My Response

Date _____

Idea, Thought, or Action

My Response

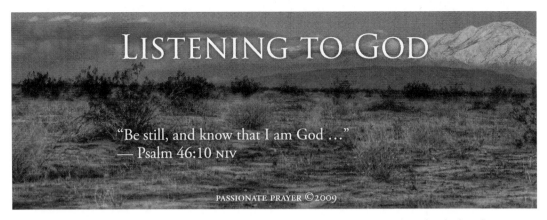

LISTENING TO GOD

"Be still, and know that I am God …"
— Psalm 46:10 NIV

PASSIONATE PRAYER ©2009

Write ideas, thoughts, and actions that come to mind during your quiet time about family, friends, ministry, prayer, quiet time, work, and encouraging others. Ask God how to act upon what you hear.

Date _____

Idea, Thought, or Action

My Response

Date _____

Idea, Thought, or Action

My Response

LISTENING TO GOD

"Be still, and know that I am God …"
— Psalm 46:10 NIV

PASSIONATE PRAYER ©2009

Write ideas, thoughts, and actions that come to mind during your quiet time about family, friends, ministry, prayer, quiet time, work, and encouraging others. Ask God how to act upon what you hear.

Date _____

Idea, Thought, or Action

My Response

Date _____

Idea, Thought, or Action

My Response

LISTENING TO GOD

"Be still, and know that I am God ..."
— Psalm 46:10 NIV

PASSIONATE PRAYER ©2009

Write ideas, thoughts, and actions that come to mind during your quiet time about family, friends, ministry, prayer, quiet time, work, and encouraging others. Ask God how to act upon what you hear.

Date _____

Idea, Thought, or Action

My Response

Date _____

Idea, Thought, or Action

My Response

LISTENING TO GOD

"Be still, and know that I am God ..."
— Psalm 46:10 NIV

PASSIONATE PRAYER ©2009

Write ideas, thoughts, and actions that come to mind during your quiet time about family, friends,
ministry, prayer, quiet time, work, and encouraging others. Ask God how to act upon what you hear.

Date _____

Idea, Thought, or Action

My Response

Date _____

Idea, Thought, or Action

My Response

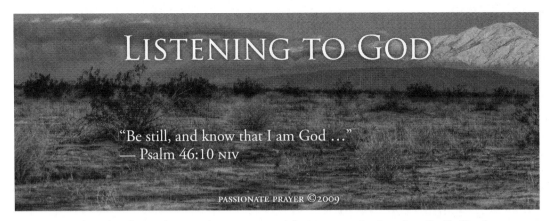

LISTENING TO GOD

"Be still, and know that I am God ..."
— Psalm 46:10 NIV

PASSIONATE PRAYER ©2009

Write ideas, thoughts, and actions that come to mind during your quiet time about family, friends, ministry, prayer, quiet time, work, and encouraging others. Ask God how to act upon what you hear.

Date _____

Idea, Thought, or Action

My Response

Date _____

Idea, Thought, or Action

My Response

LISTENING TO GOD

"Be still, and know that I am God …"
— Psalm 46:10 NIV

Write ideas, thoughts, and actions that come to mind during your quiet time about family, friends, ministry, prayer, quiet time, work, and encouraging others. Ask God how to act upon what you hear.

Date _____

Idea, Thought, or Action

My Response

Date _____

Idea, Thought, or Action

My Response

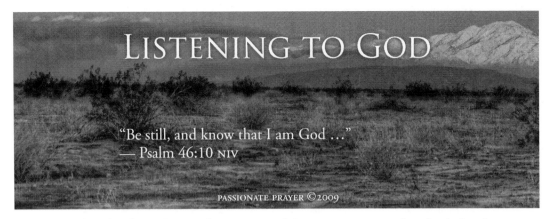

LISTENING TO GOD

"Be still, and know that I am God ..."
— Psalm 46:10 NIV

PASSIONATE PRAYER ©2009

Write ideas, thoughts, and actions that come to mind during your quiet time about family, friends, ministry, prayer, quiet time, work, and encouraging others. Ask God how to act upon what you hear.

Date _____

Idea, Thought, or Action

My Response

Date _____

Idea, Thought, or Action

My Response

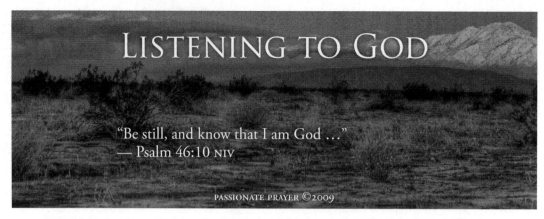

LISTENING TO GOD

"Be still, and know that I am God …"
— Psalm 46:10 NIV

Write ideas, thoughts, and actions that come to mind during your quiet time about family, friends, ministry, prayer, quiet time, work, and encouraging others. Ask God how to act upon what you hear.

Date _____

Idea, Thought, or Action

My Response

Date _____

Idea, Thought, or Action

My Response

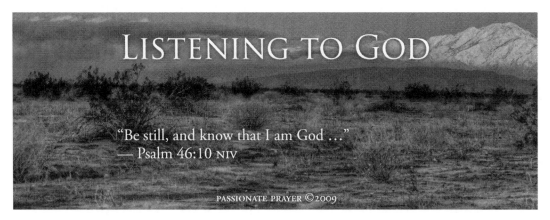

LISTENING TO GOD

"Be still, and know that I am God ..."
— Psalm 46:10 NIV

Write ideas, thoughts, and actions that come to mind during your quiet time about family, friends, ministry, prayer, quiet time, work, and encouraging others. Ask God how to act upon what you hear.

Date _____

Idea, Thought, or Action

My Response

Date _____

Idea, Thought, or Action

My Response

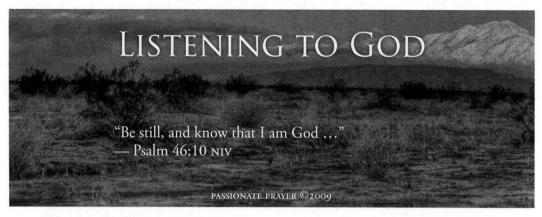

LISTENING TO GOD

"Be still, and know that I am God ..."
— Psalm 46:10 NIV

PASSIONATE PRAYER ©2009

Write ideas, thoughts, and actions that come to mind during your quiet time about family, friends, ministry, prayer, quiet time, work, and encouraging others. Ask God how to act upon what you hear.

Date _____

Idea, Thought, or Action

My Response

Date _____

Idea, Thought, or Action

My Response

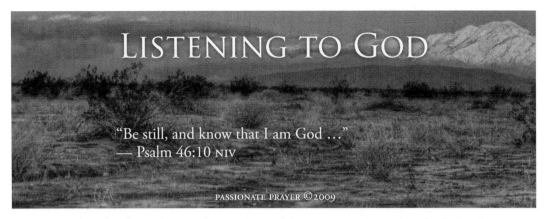

LISTENING TO GOD

"Be still, and know that I am God ..."
— Psalm 46:10 NIV

PASSIONATE PRAYER ©2009

Write ideas, thoughts, and actions that come to mind during your quiet time about family, friends, ministry, prayer, quiet time, work, and encouraging others. Ask God how to act upon what you hear.

Date _____

Idea, Thought, or Action

My Response

Date _____

Idea, Thought, or Action

My Response

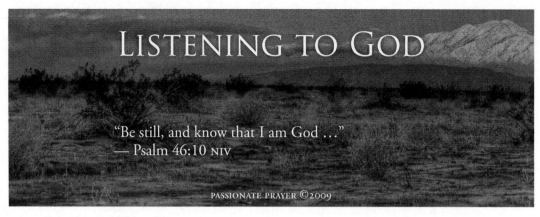

LISTENING TO GOD

"Be still, and know that I am God …"
— Psalm 46:10 NIV

PASSIONATE PRAYER ©2009

Write ideas, thoughts, and actions that come to mind during your quiet time about family, friends, ministry, prayer, quiet time, work, and encouraging others. Ask God how to act upon what you hear.

Date _____

Idea, Thought, or Action

My Response

Date _____

Idea, Thought, or Action

My Response

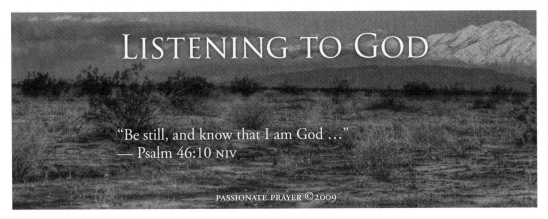

LISTENING TO GOD

"Be still, and know that I am God ..."
— Psalm 46:10 NIV

PASSIONATE PRAYER ©2009

Write ideas, thoughts, and actions that come to mind during your quiet time about family, friends, ministry, prayer, quiet time, work, and encouraging others. Ask God how to act upon what you hear.

Date _____

Idea, Thought, or Action

My Response

Date _____

Idea, Thought, or Action

My Response

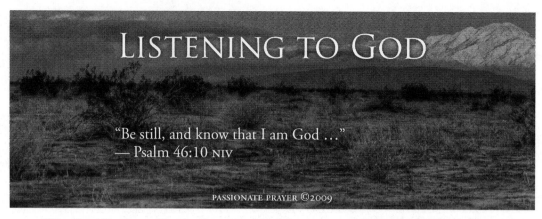

LISTENING TO GOD

"Be still, and know that I am God ..."
— Psalm 46:10 NIV

PASSIONATE PRAYER ©2009

Write ideas, thoughts, and actions that come to mind during your quiet time about family, friends, ministry, prayer, quiet time, work, and encouraging others. Ask God how to act upon what you hear.

Date _____

Idea, Thought, or Action

My Response

Date _____

Idea, Thought, or Action

My Response

THANK YOU, LORD

"One of them, when he saw he was healed, came back, praising God in a loud voice. He threw himself at Jesus' feet and thanked him ..." — Luke 17:15-16 NIV

Every day, try to write at least one thing you thank God for in your life.

Date	Lord, I am thankful for ...

THANK YOU, LORD

"One of them, when he saw he was healed, came back, praising God in a loud voice. He threw himself at Jesus' feet and thanked him ..." — Luke 17:15-16 NIV

Every day, try to write at least one thing you thank God for in your life.

Date	*Lord, I am thankful for ...*

THANK YOU, LORD

"One of them, when he saw he was healed, came back, praising God in a loud voice. He threw himself at Jesus' feet and thanked him ..." — Luke 17:15-16 NIV

Every day, try to write at least one thing you thank God for in your life.

Date	Lord, I am thankful for ...

THANK YOU, LORD

"One of them, when he saw he was healed, came back, praising God in a loud voice. He threw himself at Jesus' feet and thanked him …" — Luke 17:15-16 NIV

PASSIONATE PRAYER ©2009

Every day, try to write at least one thing you thank God for in your life.

Date   *Lord, I am thankful for …*

THANK YOU, LORD

"One of them, when he saw he was healed, came back, praising God in a loud voice. He threw himself at Jesus' feet and thanked him …" — Luke 17:15-16 NIV

PASSIONATE PRAYER ©2009

Every day, try to write at least one thing you thank God for in your life.

Date   *Lord, I am thankful for …*

THANK YOU, LORD

"One of them, when he saw he was healed, came back, praising God in a loud voice. He threw himself at Jesus' feet and thanked him ..." — Luke 17:15-16 NIV

PASSIONATE PRAYER ©2009

Every day, try to write at least one thing you thank God for in your life.

Date	Lord, I am thankful for ...

THANK YOU, LORD

"One of them, when he saw he was healed, came back, praising God in a loud voice. He threw himself at Jesus' feet and thanked him ..." — Luke 17:15-16 NIV

PASSIONATE PRAYER ©2009

Every day, try to write at least one thing you thank God for in your life.

Date	Lord, I am thankful for ...

THANK YOU, LORD

"One of them, when he saw he was healed, came back, praising God in a loud voice. He threw himself at Jesus' feet and thanked him ..." — Luke 17:15-16 NIV

PASSIONATE PRAYER ©2009

Every day, try to write at least one thing you thank God for in your life.

Date   *Lord, I am thankful for ...*

THANK YOU, LORD

"One of them, when he saw he was healed, came back, praising God in a loud voice. He threw himself at Jesus' feet and thanked him ..." — Luke 17:15-16 NIV

PASSIONATE PRAYER ©2009

Every day, try to write at least one thing you thank God for in your life.

Date	*Lord, I am thankful for ...*

Thank You, Lord

"One of them, when he saw he was healed, came back, praising God in a loud voice. He threw himself at Jesus' feet and thanked him ..." — Luke 17:15-16 NIV

PASSIONATE PRAYER ©2009

Every day, try to write at least one thing you thank God for in your life.

Date   **Lord, I am thankful for ...**

THANK YOU, LORD

"One of them, when he saw he was healed, came back, praising God in a loud voice. He threw himself at Jesus' feet and thanked him ..." — Luke 17:15-16 NIV

PASSIONATE PRAYER ©2009

Every day, try to write at least one thing you thank God for in your life.

Date   *Lord, I am thankful for ...*

THANK YOU, LORD

"One of them, when he saw he was healed, came back, praising God in a loud voice. He threw himself at Jesus' feet and thanked him …" — Luke 17:15-16 NIV

PASSIONATE PRAYER ©2009

Every day, try to write at least one thing you thank God for in your life.

Date	Lord, I am thankful for …

THANK YOU, LORD

"One of them, when he saw he was healed, came back, praising God in a loud voice. He threw himself at Jesus' feet and thanked him …" — Luke 17:15-16 NIV

PASSIONATE PRAYER ©2009

Every day, try to write at least one thing you thank God for in your life.

Date   *Lord, I am thankful for …*

Thank You, Lord

"One of them, when he saw he was healed, came back, praising God in a loud voice. He threw himself at Jesus' feet and thanked him ..." — Luke 17:15-16 NIV

Every day, try to write at least one thing you thank God for in your life.

Date	Lord, I am thankful for ...

THANK YOU, LORD

"One of them, when he saw he was healed, came back, praising God in a loud voice. He threw himself at Jesus' feet and thanked him ..." — Luke 17:15-16 NIV

PASSIONATE PRAYER ©2009

Every day, try to write at least one thing you thank God for in your life.

Date   *Lord, I am thankful for ...*

THANK YOU, LORD

"One of them, when he saw he was healed, came back, praising God in a loud voice. He threw himself at Jesus' feet and thanked him …" — Luke 17:15-16 NIV

PASSIONATE PRAYER ©2009

Every day, try to write at least one thing you thank God for in your life.

Date   **Lord, I am thankful for …**

THANK YOU, LORD

"One of them, when he saw he was healed, came back, praising God in a loud voice. He threw himself at Jesus' feet and thanked him ..." — Luke 17:15-16 NIV

PASSIONATE PRAYER ©2009

Every day, try to write at least one thing you thank God for in your life.

Date	Lord, I am thankful for ...

THANK YOU, LORD

"One of them, when he saw he was healed, came back, praising God in a loud voice. He threw himself at Jesus' feet and thanked him …" — Luke 17:15-16 NIV

PASSIONATE PRAYER ©2009

Every day, try to write at least one thing you thank God for in your life.

Date   **Lord, I am thankful for …**

THANK YOU, LORD

"One of them, when he saw he was healed, came back, praising God in a loud voice. He threw himself at Jesus' feet and thanked him ..." — Luke 17:15-16 NIV

PASSIONATE PRAYER ©2009

Every day, try to write at least one thing you thank God for in your life.

Date   *Lord, I am thankful for ...*

THANK YOU, LORD

"One of them, when he saw he was healed, came back, praising God in a loud voice. He threw himself at Jesus' feet and thanked him ..." — Luke 17:15-16 NIV

Every day, try to write at least one thing you thank God for in your life.

Date   *Lord, I am thankful for ...*

THANK YOU, LORD

"One of them, when he saw he was healed, came back, praising God in a loud voice. He threw himself at Jesus' feet and thanked him ..." — Luke 17:15-16 NIV

PASSIONATE PRAYER ©2009

Every day, try to write at least one thing you thank God for in your life.

Date	*Lord, I am thankful for ...*

THANK YOU, LORD

"One of them, when he saw he was healed, came back, praising God in a loud voice. He threw himself at Jesus' feet and thanked him ..." — Luke 17:15-16 NIV

Every day, try to write at least one thing you thank God for in your life.

Date   *Lord, I am thankful for ...*

THANK YOU, LORD

"One of them, when he saw he was healed, came back, praising God in a loud voice. He threw himself at Jesus' feet and thanked him …" — Luke 17:15-16 NIV

PASSIONATE PRAYER ©2009.

Every day, try to write at least one thing you thank God for in your life.

Date   Lord, I am thankful for …

THANK YOU, LORD

"One of them, when he saw he was healed, came back, praising God in a loud voice. He threw himself at Jesus' feet and thanked him ..." — Luke 17:15-16 NIV

PASSIONATE PRAYER ©2009

Every day, try to write at least one thing you thank God for in your life.

Date	Lord, I am thankful for ...

Thank You, Lord

"One of them, when he saw he was healed, came back, praising God in a loud voice. He threw himself at Jesus' feet and thanked him ..." — Luke 17:15-16 NIV

Every day, try to write at least one thing you thank God for in your life.

Date	Lord, I am thankful for ...

THANK YOU, LORD

"One of them, when he saw he was healed, came back, praising God in a loud voice. He threw himself at Jesus' feet and thanked him …" — Luke 17:15-16 NIV

Every day, try to write at least one thing you thank God for in your life.

Date	Lord, I am thankful for …

THANK YOU, LORD

"One of them, when he saw he was healed, came back, praising God in a loud voice. He threw himself at Jesus' feet and thanked him ..." — Luke 17:15-16 NIV

PASSIONATE PRAYER ©2009

Every day, try to write at least one thing you thank God for in your life.

Date   *Lord, I am thankful for ...*

THANK YOU, LORD

"One of them, when he saw he was healed, came back, praising God in a loud voice. He threw himself at Jesus' feet and thanked him ..." — Luke 17:15-16 NIV

PASSIONATE PRAYER ©2009

Every day, try to write at least one thing you thank God for in your life.

Date	Lord, I am thankful for ...

THANK YOU, LORD

"One of them, when he saw he was healed, came back, praising God in a loud voice. He threw himself at Jesus' feet and thanked him …" — Luke 17:15-16 NIV

Every day, try to write at least one thing you thank God for in your life.

Date   *Lord, I am thankful for …*

THANK YOU, LORD

"One of them, when he saw he was healed, came back, praising God in a loud voice. He threw himself at Jesus' feet and thanked him ..." — Luke 17:15-16 NIV

Every day, try to write at least one thing you thank God for in your life.

Date

Lord, I am thankful for ...

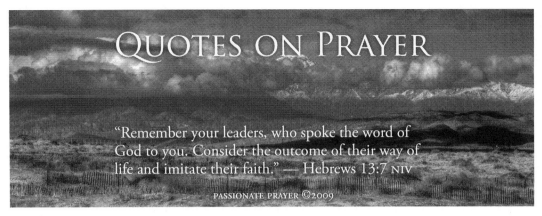

QUOTES ON PRAYER

"Remember your leaders, who spoke the word of God to you. Consider the outcome of their way of life and imitate their faith." — Hebrews 13:7 NIV

PASSIONATE PRAYER ©2009

Record significant quotes and include author, source, and page numbers.

Source _____

Source _____

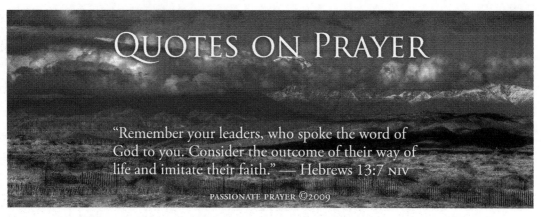

QUOTES ON PRAYER

"Remember your leaders, who spoke the word of
God to you. Consider the outcome of their way of
life and imitate their faith." — Hebrews 13:7 NIV

PASSIONATE PRAYER ©2009

Record significant quotes and include author, source, and page numbers.

Source _____

Source _____

QUOTES ON PRAYER

"Remember your leaders, who spoke the word of God to you. Consider the outcome of their way of life and imitate their faith." — Hebrews 13:7 NIV

PASSIONATE PRAYER ©2009

Record significant quotes and include author, source, and page numbers.

Source _____

Source _____

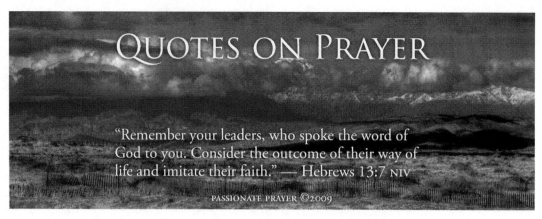

QUOTES ON PRAYER

"Remember your leaders, who spoke the word of
God to you. Consider the outcome of their way of
life and imitate their faith." — Hebrews 13:7 NIV

PASSIONATE PRAYER ©2009

Record significant quotes and include author, source, and page numbers.

Source _____

Source _____

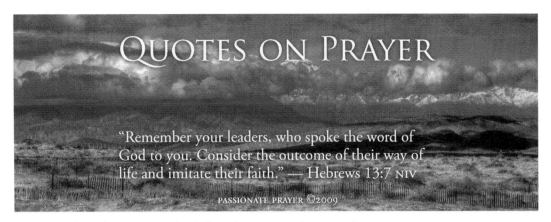

QUOTES ON PRAYER

"Remember your leaders, who spoke the word of God to you. Consider the outcome of their way of life and imitate their faith." — Hebrews 13:7 NIV

PASSIONATE PRAYER ©2009

Record significant quotes and include author, source, and page numbers.

Source _____

Source _____

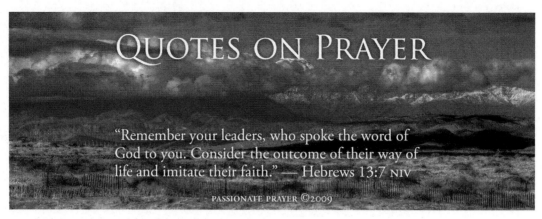

QUOTES ON PRAYER

"Remember your leaders, who spoke the word of God to you. Consider the outcome of their way of life and imitate their faith." — Hebrews 13:7 NIV

PASSIONATE PRAYER ©2009

Record significant quotes and include author, source, and page numbers.

Source _____

Source _____

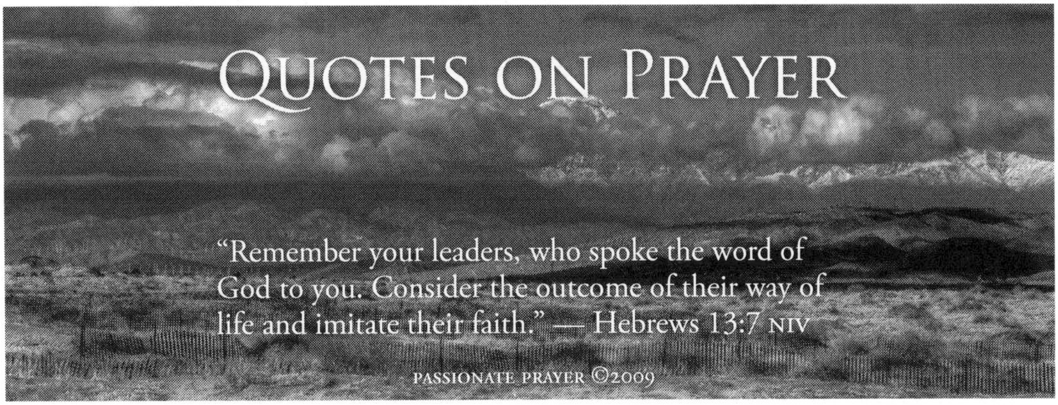

QUOTES ON PRAYER
"Remember your leaders, who spoke the word of God to you. Consider the outcome of their way of life and imitate their faith." — Hebrews 13:7 NIV
PASSIONATE PRAYER ©2009

Record significant quotes and include author, source, and page numbers.

Source ______________________________

Source ______________________________

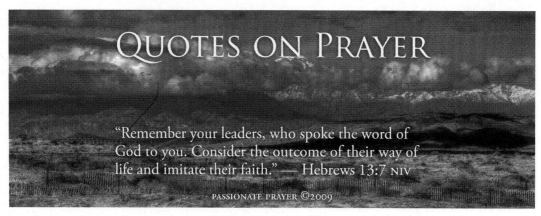

QUOTES ON PRAYER

"Remember your leaders, who spoke the word of
God to you. Consider the outcome of their way of
life and imitate their faith." — Hebrews 13:7 NIV

PASSIONATE PRAYER ©2009

Record significant quotes and include author, source, and page numbers.

Source _____

Source _____

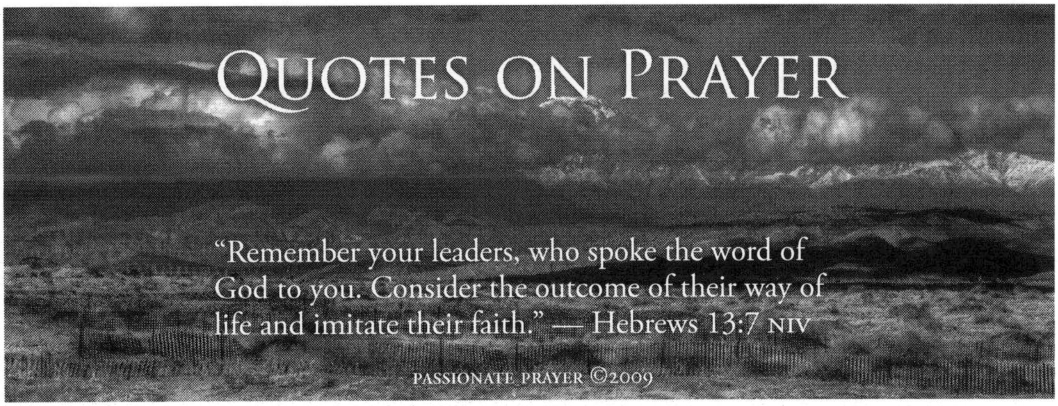

QUOTES ON PRAYER
"Remember your leaders, who spoke the word of God to you. Consider the outcome of their way of life and imitate their faith." — Hebrews 13:7 NIV
PASSIONATE PRAYER ©2009

Record significant quotes and include author, source, and page numbers.

Source ______________________________

Source ______________________________

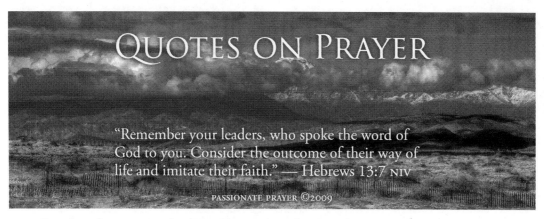

QUOTES ON PRAYER

"Remember your leaders, who spoke the word of God to you. Consider the outcome of their way of life and imitate their faith." — Hebrews 13:7 NIV

PASSIONATE PRAYER ©2009

Record significant quotes and include author, source, and page numbers.

Source _____

Source _____

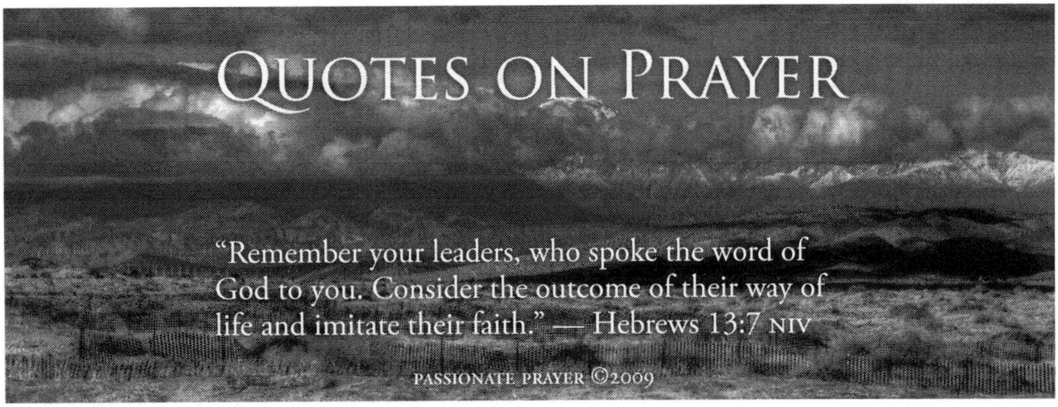

QUOTES ON PRAYER

"Remember your leaders, who spoke the word of God to you. Consider the outcome of their way of life and imitate their faith." — Hebrews 13:7 NIV

PASSIONATE PRAYER ©2009

Record significant quotes and include author, source, and page numbers.

Source _____

Source _____

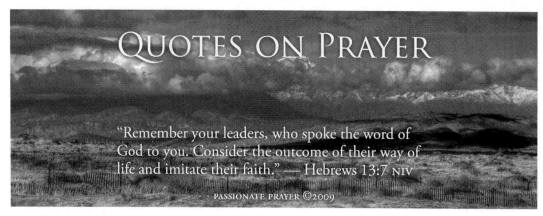

QUOTES ON PRAYER

"Remember your leaders, who spoke the word of God to you. Consider the outcome of their way of life and imitate their faith." — Hebrews 13:7 NIV

PASSIONATE PRAYER ©2009

Record significant quotes and include author, source, and page numbers.

Source _____

Source _____

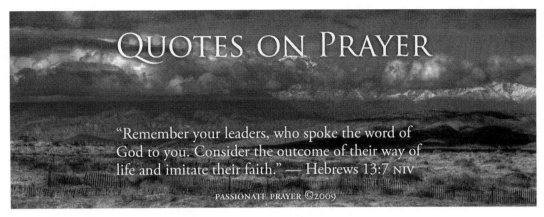

QUOTES ON PRAYER

"Remember your leaders, who spoke the word of God to you. Consider the outcome of their way of life and imitate their faith." — Hebrews 13:7 NIV

PASSIONATE PRAYER ©2009

Record significant quotes and include author, source, and page numbers.

Source _____

Source _____

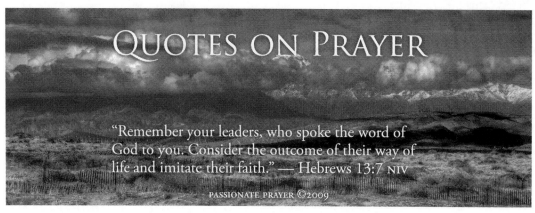

QUOTES ON PRAYER

"Remember your leaders, who spoke the word of
God to you. Consider the outcome of their way of
life and imitate their faith." — Hebrews 13:7 NIV

PASSIONATE PRAYER ©2009

Record significant quotes and include author, source, and page numbers.

Source _____

Source _____

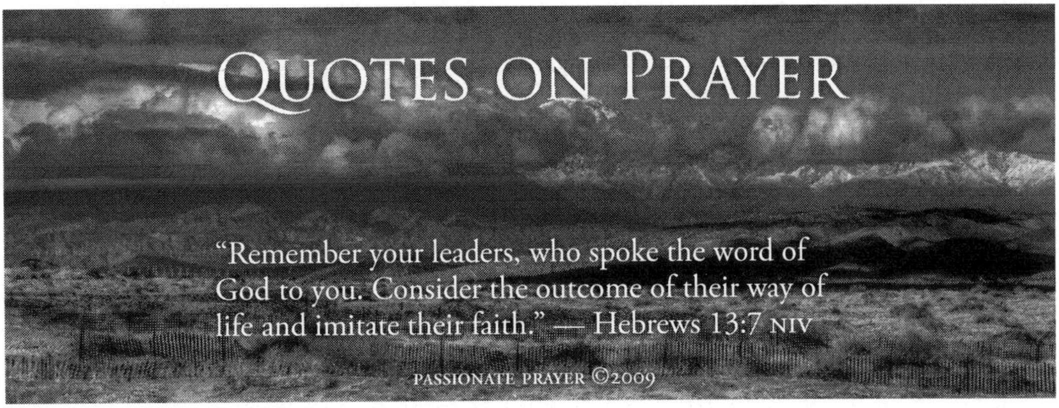

QUOTES ON PRAYER
"Remember your leaders, who spoke the word of God to you. Consider the outcome of their way of life and imitate their faith." — Hebrews 13:7 NIV
PASSIONATE PRAYER ©2009

Record significant quotes and include author, source, and page numbers.

Source ______________________________

Source ______________________________

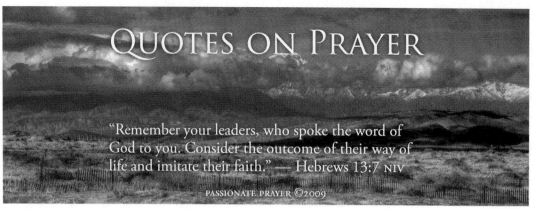

QUOTES ON PRAYER

"Remember your leaders, who spoke the word of God to you. Consider the outcome of their way of life and imitate their faith." — Hebrews 13:7 NIV

PASSIONATE PRAYER ©2009

Record significant quotes and include author, source, and page numbers.

Source ————————————————————————————

Source ————————————————————————————

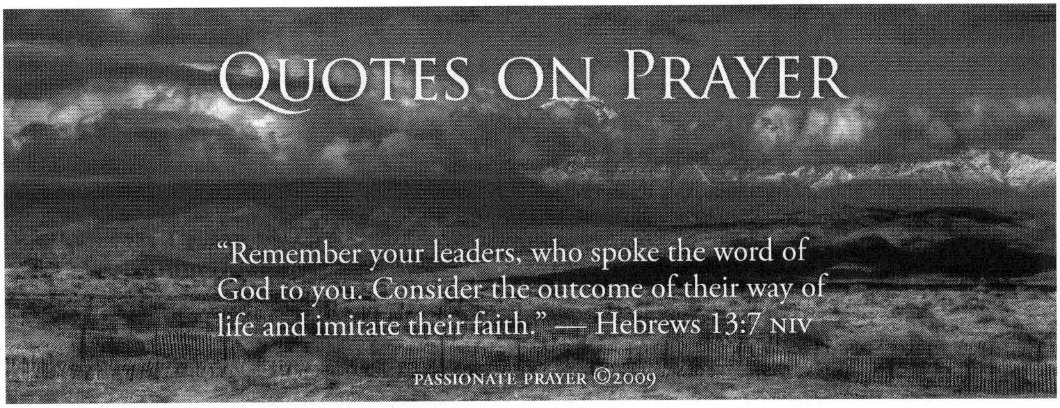

QUOTES ON PRAYER
"Remember your leaders, who spoke the word of God to you. Consider the outcome of their way of life and imitate their faith." — Hebrews 13:7 NIV
PASSIONATE PRAYER ©2009

Record significant quotes and include author, source, and page numbers.

Source ____

Source ____

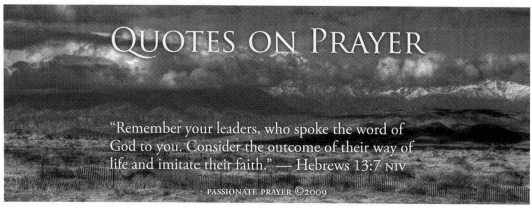

QUOTES ON PRAYER

"Remember your leaders, who spoke the word of God to you. Consider the outcome of their way of life and imitate their faith." — Hebrews 13:7 NIV

PASSIONATE PRAYER ©2009

Record significant quotes and include author, source, and page numbers.

Source _____

Source _____

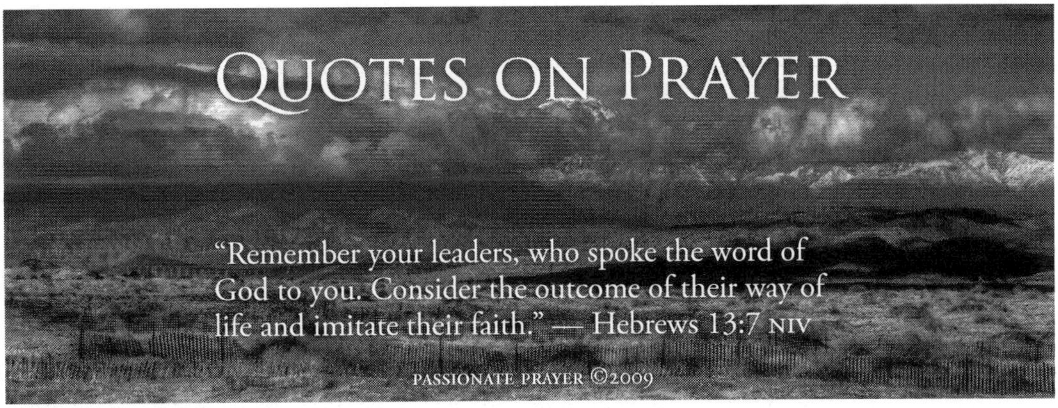

QUOTES ON PRAYER
"Remember your leaders, who spoke the word of God to you. Consider the outcome of their way of life and imitate their faith." — Hebrews 13:7 NIV
PASSIONATE PRAYER ©2009

Record significant quotes and include author, source, and page numbers.

Source ____

Source ____

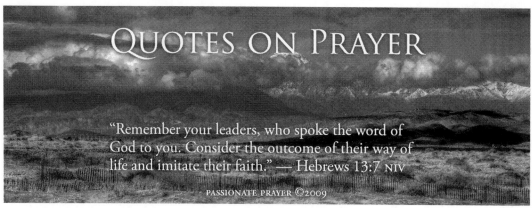

Quotes on Prayer

"Remember your leaders, who spoke the word of God to you. Consider the outcome of their way of life and imitate their faith." — Hebrews 13:7 NIV

PASSIONATE PRAYER ©2009

Record significant quotes and include author, source, and page numbers.

Source _____

Source _____

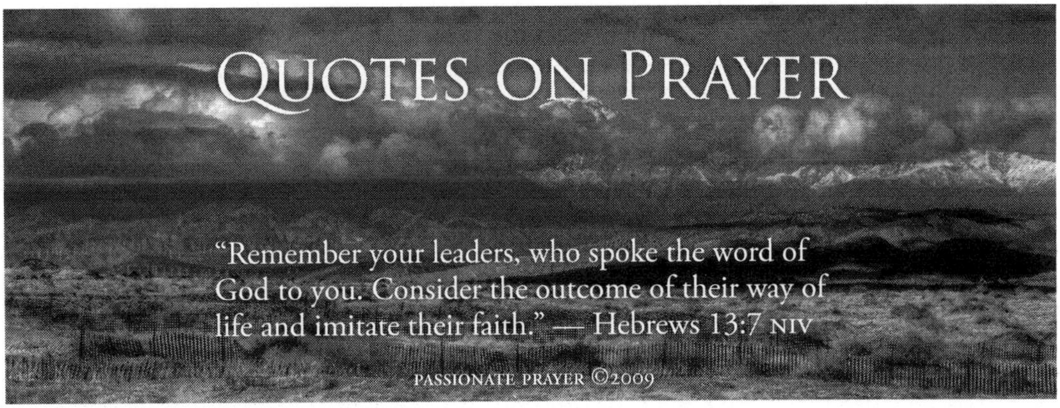

QUOTES ON PRAYER

"Remember your leaders, who spoke the word of
God to you. Consider the outcome of their way of
life and imitate their faith." — Hebrews 13:7 NIV

PASSIONATE PRAYER ©2009

Record significant quotes and include author, source, and page numbers.

Source _____

Source _____

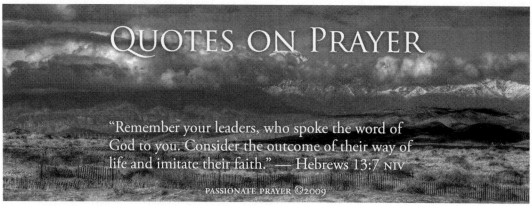

QUOTES ON PRAYER

"Remember your leaders, who spoke the word of
God to you. Consider the outcome of their way of
life and imitate their faith." — Hebrews 13:7 NIV

PASSIONATE PRAYER ©2009

Record significant quotes and include author, source, and page numbers.

Source _____

Source _____

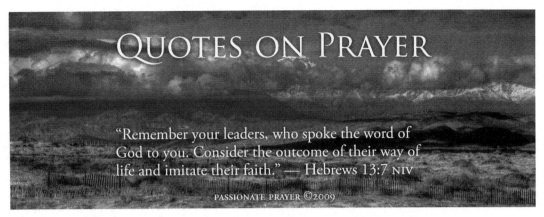

QUOTES ON PRAYER

"Remember your leaders, who spoke the word of
God to you. Consider the outcome of their way of
life and imitate their faith." — Hebrews 13:7 NIV

PASSIONATE PRAYER ©2009

Record significant quotes and include author, source, and page numbers.

Source _____

Source _____

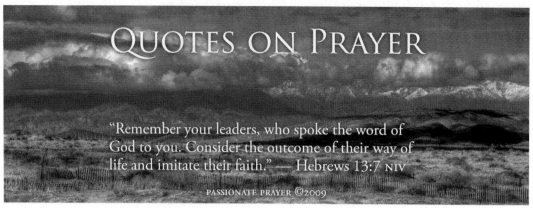

QUOTES ON PRAYER

"Remember your leaders, who spoke the word of
God to you. Consider the outcome of their way of
life and imitate their faith." — Hebrews 13:7 NIV

PASSIONATE PRAYER ©2009

Record significant quotes and include author, source, and page numbers.

Source _____

Source _____

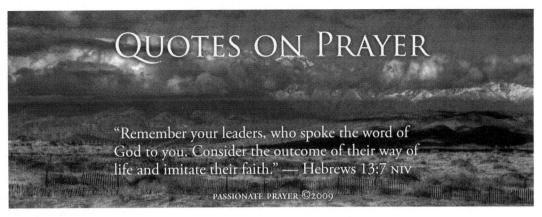

QUOTES ON PRAYER

"Remember your leaders, who spoke the word of God to you. Consider the outcome of their way of life and imitate their faith." — Hebrews 13:7 NIV

PASSIONATE PRAYER ©2009

Record significant quotes and include author, source, and page numbers.

Source _____

Source _____

QUOTES ON PRAYER

"Remember your leaders, who spoke the word of God to you. Consider the outcome of their way of life and imitate their faith." — Hebrews 13:7 NIV

PASSIONATE PRAYER ©2009

Record significant quotes and include author, source, and page numbers.

Source _____

Source _____

QUOTES ON PRAYER

"Remember your leaders, who spoke the word of
God to you. Consider the outcome of their way of
life and imitate their faith." — Hebrews 13:7 NIV

PASSIONATE PRAYER ©2009

Record significant quotes and include author, source, and page numbers.

Source _____

Source _____

205

Quotes on Prayer

"Remember your leaders, who spoke the word of God to you. Consider the outcome of their way of life and imitate their faith." — Hebrews 13:7 NIV

Record significant quotes and include author, source, and page numbers.

Source _____

Source _____

QUOTES ON PRAYER

"Remember your leaders, who spoke the word of God to you. Consider the outcome of their way of life and imitate their faith." — Hebrews 13:7 NIV

PASSIONATE PRAYER ©2009

Record significant quotes and include author, source, and page numbers.

Source _____

Source _____

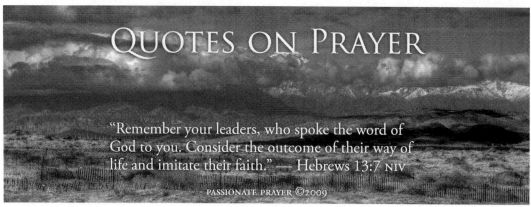

QUOTES ON PRAYER

"Remember your leaders, who spoke the word of God to you. Consider the outcome of their way of life and imitate their faith." — Hebrews 13:7 NIV

PASSIONATE PRAYER ©2009

Record significant quotes and include author, source, and page numbers.

Source _____

Source _____

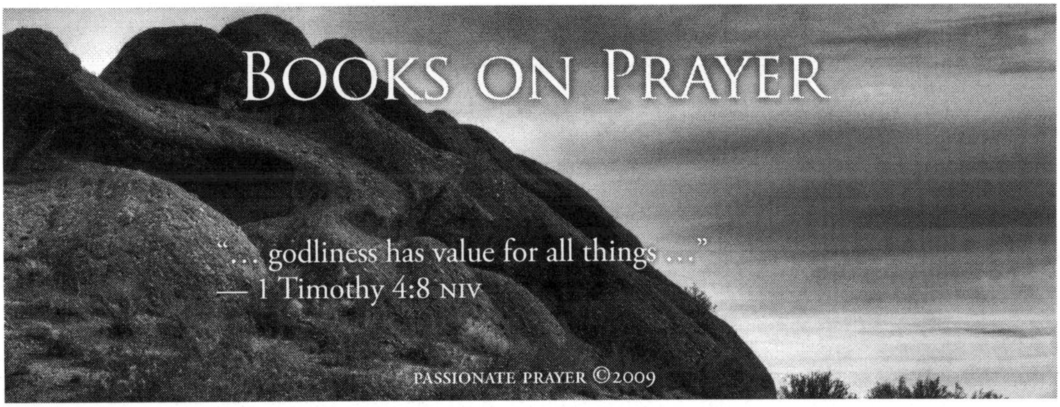

BOOKS ON PRAYER

"... godliness has value for all things ..."
— 1 Timothy 4:8 NIV

PASSIONATE PRAYER ©2009

As you read books on prayer, underlining important quotes, record page numbers with a subject–quote.

Date _____

Book _____ Author _____

Page(s)   Subject—Quote

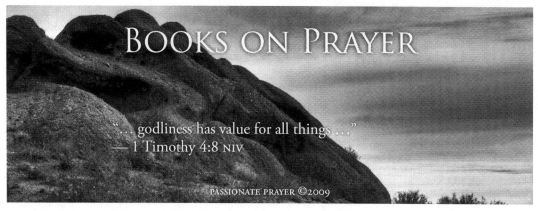

BOOKS ON PRAYER

"... godliness has value for all things ..."
— 1 Timothy 4:8 NIV

PASSIONATE PRAYER ©2009

As you read books on prayer, underlining important quotes, record page numbers with a subject—quote.

Date _____

Book _____ *Author* _____

Page(s)	*Subject—Quote*

BOOKS ON PRAYER

"...godliness has value for all things..."
— 1 Timothy 4:8 NIV

PASSIONATE PRAYER ©2009

As you read books on prayer, underlining important quotes, record page numbers with a subject–quote.

Date _____

Book _____ Author _____

Page(s)	Subject—Quote

BOOKS ON PRAYER

"...godliness has value for all things..."
— 1 Timothy 4:8 NIV

PASSIONATE PRAYER ©2009

As you read books on prayer, underlining important quotes, record page numbers with a subject–quote.

Date _____

Book _____ Author _____

Page(s)	Subject—Quote

BOOKS ON PRAYER

"... godliness has value for all things ..."
— 1 Timothy 4:8 NIV

As you read books on prayer, underlining important quotes, record page numbers with a subject–quote.

Date _____

Book _____ Author _____

Page(s)	Subject—Quote

BOOKS ON PRAYER

"...godliness has value for all things..."
— 1 Timothy 4:8 NIV

As you read books on prayer, underlining important quotes, record page numbers with a subject–quote.

Date _____

Book _____ Author _____

Page(s)	Subject—Quote

BOOKS ON PRAYER

"... godliness has value for all things ..."
— 1 Timothy 4:8 NIV

PASSIONATE PRAYER ©2009

As you read books on prayer, underlining important quotes, record page numbers with a subject–quote.

Date _____

Book _____ Author _____

Page(s)   Subject—Quote

BOOKS ON PRAYER

"...godliness has value for all things..."
— 1 Timothy 4:8 NIV

PASSIONATE PRAYER ©2009

As you read books on prayer, underlining important quotes, record page numbers with a subject–quote.

Date _____

Book _____ Author _____

Page(s)	Subject—Quote

BOOKS ON PRAYER

"... godliness has value for all things ..."
— 1 Timothy 4:8 NIV

PASSIONATE PRAYER ©2009

As you read books on prayer, underlining important quotes, record page numbers with a subject–quote.

Date _____

Book _____ Author _____

Page(s)   Subject—Quote

BOOKS ON PRAYER

"... godliness has value for all things ..."
— 1 Timothy 4:8 NIV

PASSIONATE PRAYER ©2009

As you read books on prayer, underlining important quotes, record page numbers with a subject—quote.

Date _____

Book _____ Author _____

Page(s)   Subject—Quote

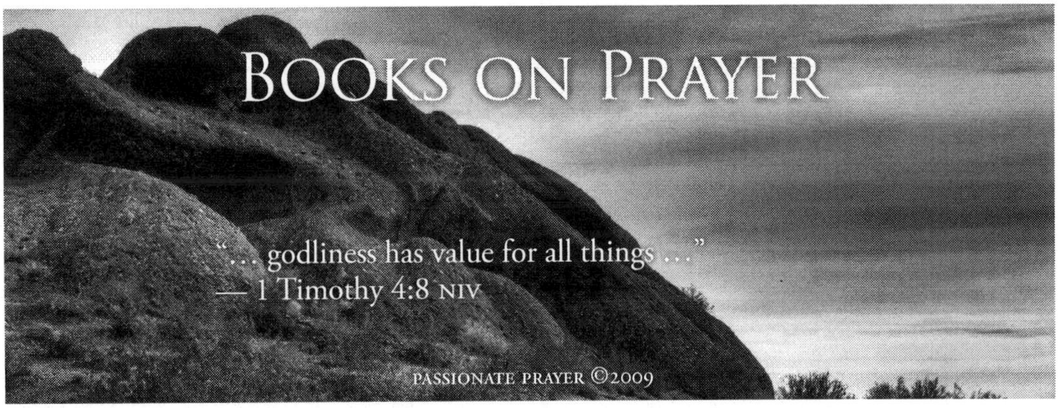

BOOKS ON PRAYER

"... godliness has value for all things ..."
— 1 Timothy 4:8 NIV

PASSIONATE PRAYER ©2009

As you read books on prayer, underlining important quotes, record page numbers with a subject–quote.

Date _____

Book _____ Author _____

Page(s)   Subject—Quote

BOOKS ON PRAYER

"...godliness has value for all things..."
— 1 Timothy 4:8 NIV

PASSIONATE PRAYER ©2009

As you read books on prayer, underlining important quotes, record page numbers with a subject—quote.

Date _____

Book _____ Author _____

Page(s)   Subject—Quote

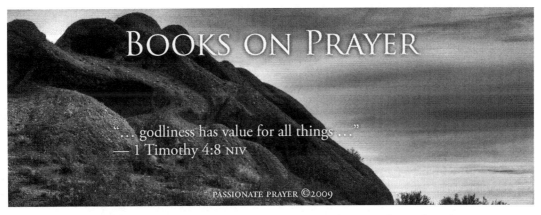

BOOKS ON PRAYER

"... godliness has value for all things ..."
— 1 Timothy 4:8 NIV

PASSIONATE PRAYER ©2009

As you read books on prayer, underlining important quotes, record page numbers with a subject–quote.

Date _____

Book _____ Author _____

Page(s)   Subject—Quote

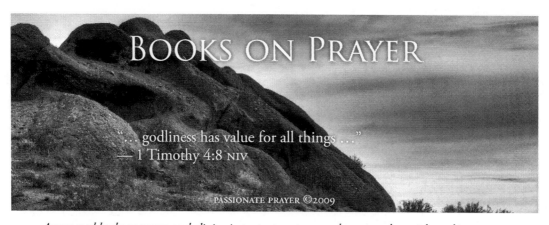

BOOKS ON PRAYER

"... godliness has value for all things ..."
— 1 Timothy 4:8 NIV

As you read books on prayer, underlining important quotes, record page numbers with a subject–quote.

Date _____

Book _____ Author _____

Page(s)	Subject—Quote

BOOKS ON PRAYER

"... godliness has value for all things ..."
— 1 Timothy 4:8 NIV

As you read books on prayer, underlining important quotes, record page numbers with a subject–quote.

Date _____

Book _____ Author _____

Page(s)	Subject—Quote

BOOKS ON PRAYER

"... godliness has value for all things ..."
— 1 Timothy 4:8 NIV

PASSIONATE PRAYER ©2009

As you read books on prayer, underlining important quotes, record page numbers with a subject–quote.

Date _____

Book _____ Author _____

Page(s)   Subject—Quote

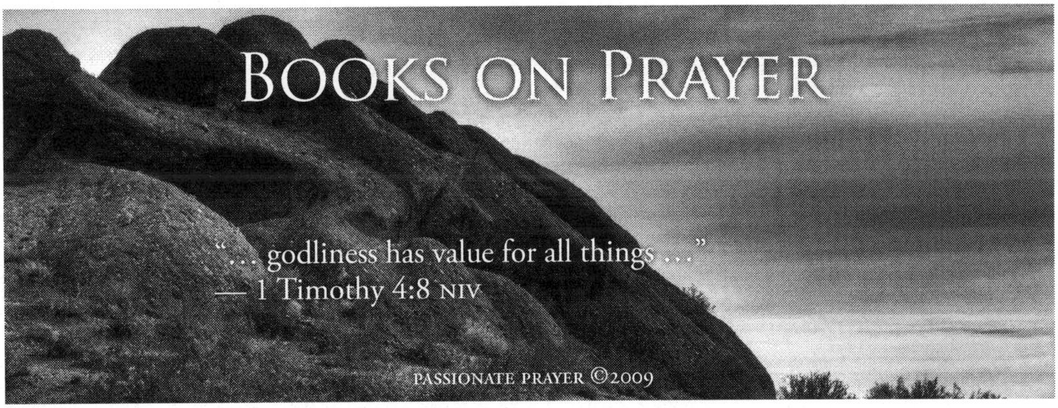

BOOKS ON PRAYER

"... godliness has value for all things ..."
— 1 Timothy 4:8 NIV

PASSIONATE PRAYER ©2009

As you read books on prayer, underlining important quotes, record page numbers with a subject—quote.

Date _____

Book _____ Author _____

Page(s)   Subject—Quote

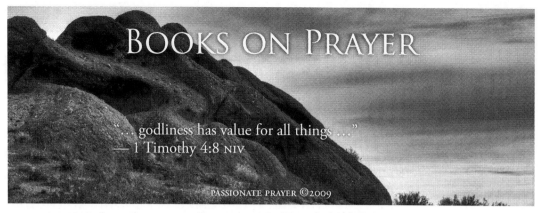

BOOKS ON PRAYER

"...godliness has value for all things..."
— 1 Timothy 4:8 NIV

PASSIONATE PRAYER ©2009

As you read books on prayer, underlining important quotes, record page numbers with a subject–quote.

Date _____

Book _____ Author _____

Page(s)	Subject—Quote

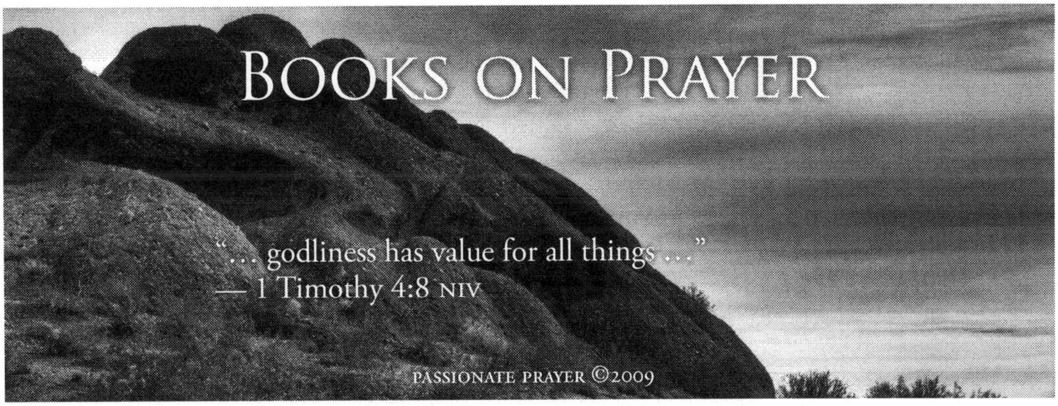

BOOKS ON PRAYER

"…godliness has value for all things…"
— 1 Timothy 4:8 NIV

PASSIONATE PRAYER ©2009

As you read books on prayer, underlining important quotes, record page numbers with a subject–quote.

Date _____

Book _____ Author _____

Page(s)	Subject—Quote

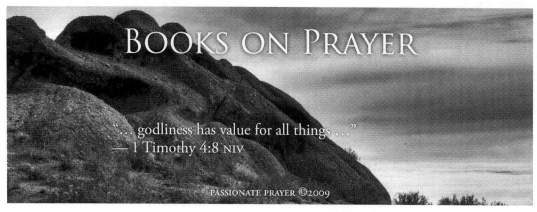

BOOKS ON PRAYER

"... godliness has value for all things ..."
— 1 Timothy 4:8 NIV

PASSIONATE PRAYER ©2009

As you read books on prayer, underlining important quotes, record page numbers with a subject–quote.

Date _____

Book _____ Author _____

Page(s)   Subject—Quote

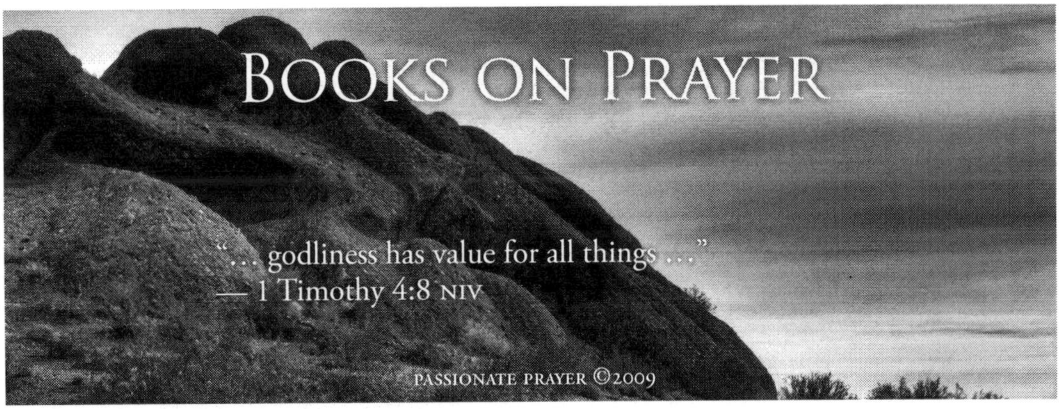

BOOKS ON PRAYER

"... godliness has value for all things ..."
— 1 Timothy 4:8 NIV

PASSIONATE PRAYER ©2009

As you read books on prayer, underlining important quotes, record page numbers with a subject–quote.

Date _____

Book _____ Author _____

Page(s)   Subject—Quote

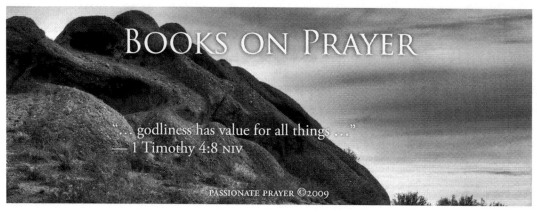

BOOKS ON PRAYER

"... godliness has value for all things ..."
— 1 Timothy 4:8 NIV

PASSIONATE PRAYER ©2009

As you read books on prayer, underlining important quotes, record page numbers with a subject—quote.

Date _____

Book _____ Author _____

Page(s)   Subject—Quote

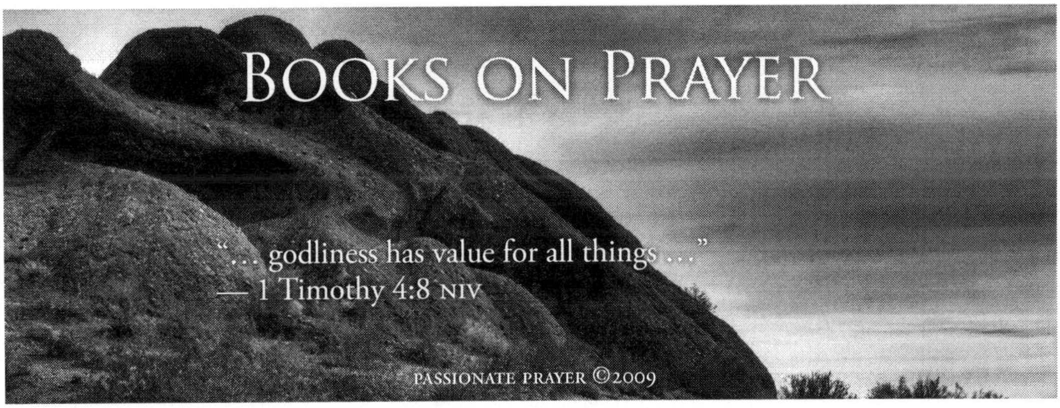

BOOKS ON PRAYER

"... godliness has value for all things ..."
— 1 Timothy 4:8 NIV

PASSIONATE PRAYER ©2009

As you read books on prayer, underlining important quotes, record page numbers with a subject–quote.

Date _____

Book _____ Author _____

Page(s)   Subject—Quote

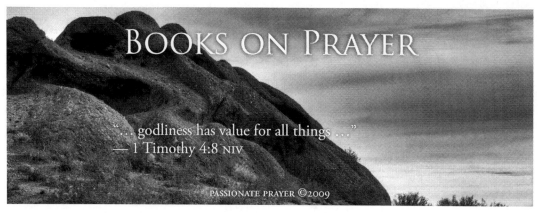

BOOKS ON PRAYER

"...godliness has value for all things ..."
— 1 Timothy 4:8 NIV

PASSIONATE PRAYER ©2009

As you read books on prayer, underlining important quotes, record page numbers with a subject—quote.

Date _____

Book _____ Author _____

Page(s)	Subject—Quote

BOOKS ON PRAYER

"... godliness has value for all things ..."
— 1 Timothy 4:8 NIV

PASSIONATE PRAYER ©2009

As you read books on prayer, underlining important quotes, record page numbers with a subject–quote.

Date _____

Book _____ Author _____

Page(s)   Subject—Quote

BOOKS ON PRAYER

"... godliness has value for all things ..."
— 1 Timothy 4:8 NIV

As you read books on prayer, underlining important quotes, record page numbers with a subject—quote.

Date _____

Book _____ Author _____

Page(s)	Subject—Quote

BOOKS ON PRAYER

"... godliness has value for all things ..."
— 1 Timothy 4:8 NIV

PASSIONATE PRAYER ©2009

As you read books on prayer, underlining important quotes, record page numbers with a subject–quote.

Date _____

Book _____ Author _____

Page(s)   Subject—Quote

BOOKS ON PRAYER

"... godliness has value for all things ..."
— 1 Timothy 4:8 NIV

PASSIONATE PRAYER ©2009

As you read books on prayer, underlining important quotes, record page numbers with a subject—quote.

Date _____

Book _____ Author _____

Page(s)	Subject—Quote

BOOKS ON PRAYER

"... godliness has value for all things ..."
— 1 Timothy 4:8 NIV

PASSIONATE PRAYER ©2009

As you read books on prayer, underlining important quotes, record page numbers with a subject–quote.

Date _____

Book _____ *Author* _____

Page(s)   *Subject—Quote*

BOOKS ON PRAYER

"...godliness has value for all things..."
— 1 Timothy 4:8 NIV

PASSIONATE PRAYER ©2009

As you read books on prayer, underlining important quotes, record page numbers with a subject–quote.

Date _____

Book _____ Author _____

Page(s)	Subject—Quote

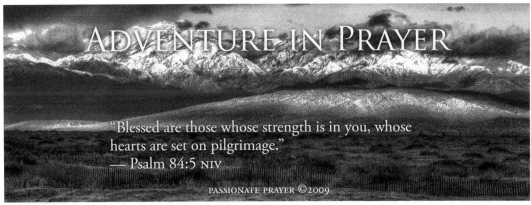

ADVENTURE IN PRAYER

*"Blessed are those whose strength is in you, whose
hearts are set on pilgrimage."*
— Psalm 84:5 NIV

PASSIONATE PRAYER ©2009

*Record your journey by writing what you are learning about prayer. Include date, key scripture &
sources, and respond in prayer to God.*

Date _____ Key Verse–Source _____

What I Am Learning

My Response

Date _____ Key Verse–Source _____

What I Am Learning

My Response

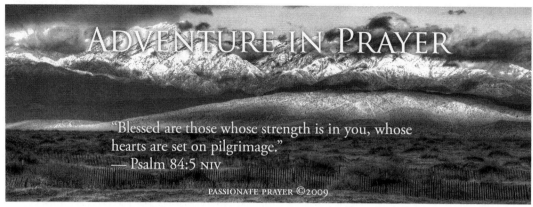

*Record your journey by writing what you are learning about prayer. Include date, key scripture &
sources, and respond in prayer to God.*

Date _____ Key Verse–Source _____

What I Am Learning

My Response

Date _____ Key Verse–Source _____

What I Am Learning

My Response

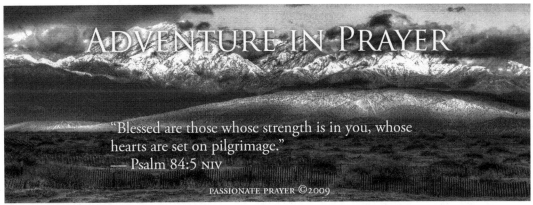

ADVENTURE IN PRAYER

"Blessed are those whose strength is in you, whose hearts are set on pilgrimage."
— Psalm 84:5 NIV

PASSIONATE PRAYER ©2009

Record your journey by writing what you are learning about prayer. Include date, key scripture & sources, and respond in prayer to God.

Date _____ Key Verse–Source _____

What I Am Learning

My Response

Date _____ Key Verse–Source _____

What I Am Learning

My Response

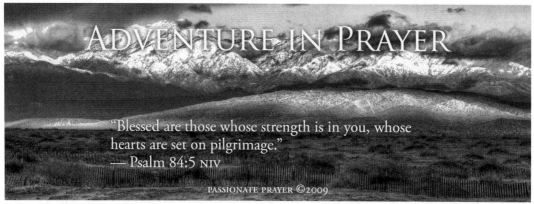

Record your journey by writing what you are learning about prayer. Include date, key scripture &
sources, and respond in prayer to God.

Date _____ Key Verse–Source _____

What I Am Learning

My Response

Date _____ Key Verse–Source _____

What I Am Learning

My Response

ADVENTURE IN PRAYER

"Blessed are those whose strength is in you, whose
hearts are set on pilgrimage."
— Psalm 84:5 NIV

Record your journey by writing what you are learning about prayer. Include date, key scripture &
sources, and respond in prayer to God.

Date _____ Key Verse–Source _____

What I Am Learning

My Response

Date _____ Key Verse–Source _____

What I Am Learning

My Response

ADVENTURE IN PRAYER

"Blessed are those whose strength is in you, whose
hearts are set on pilgrimage."
— Psalm 84:5 NIV

PASSIONATE PRAYER ©2009

*Record your journey by writing what you are learning about prayer. Include date, key scripture &
sources, and respond in prayer to God.*

Date _____ Key Verse–Source _____

What I Am Learning

My Response

Date _____ Key Verse–Source _____

What I Am Learning

My Response

ADVENTURE IN PRAYER

"Blessed are those whose strength is in you, whose
hearts are set on pilgrimage."
— Psalm 84:5 NIV

Record your journey by writing what you are learning about prayer. Include date, key scripture &
sources, and respond in prayer to God.

Date _____ Key Verse–Source _____

What I Am Learning

My Response

Date _____ Key Verse–Source _____

What I Am Learning

My Response

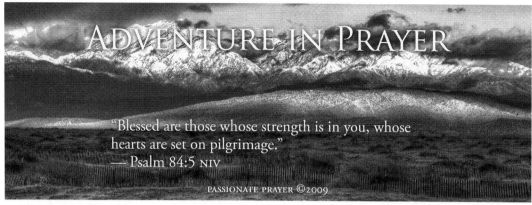

Adventure in Prayer

"Blessed are those whose strength is in you, whose
hearts are set on pilgrimage."
— Psalm 84:5 NIV

PASSIONATE PRAYER ©2009

*Record your journey by writing what you are learning about prayer. Include date, key scripture &
sources, and respond in prayer to God.*

Date _____ Key Verse–Source _____

What I Am Learning

My Response

Date _____ Key Verse–Source _____

What I Am Learning

My Response

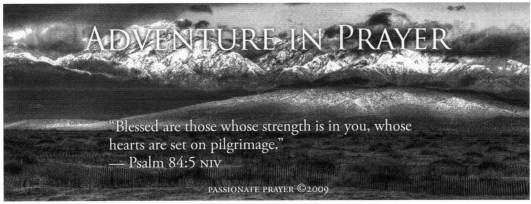

PASSIONATE PRAYER ©2009

Record your journey by writing what you are learning about prayer. Include date, key scripture &
sources, and respond in prayer to God.

Date _____ *Key Verse–Source* _____

What I Am Learning

My Response

Date _____ *Key Verse–Source* _____

What I Am Learning

My Response

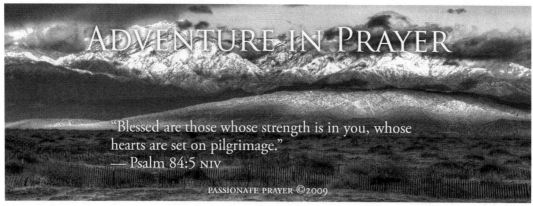

ADVENTURE IN PRAYER

"Blessed are those whose strength is in you, whose
hearts are set on pilgrimage."
— Psalm 84:5 NIV

PASSIONATE PRAYER ©2009

Record your journey by writing what you are learning about prayer. Include date, key scripture &
sources, and respond in prayer to God.

Date _____ Key Verse–Source _____

What I Am Learning

My Response

Date _____ Key Verse–Source _____

What I Am Learning

My Response

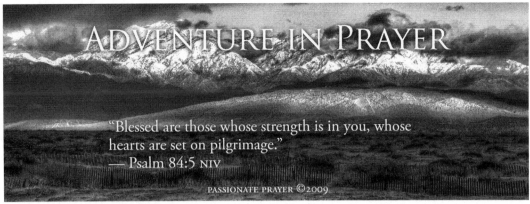

ADVENTURE IN PRAYER

"Blessed are those whose strength is in you, whose hearts are set on pilgrimage."
— Psalm 84:5 NIV

PASSIONATE PRAYER ©2009

Record your journey by writing what you are learning about prayer. Include date, key scripture &
sources, and respond in prayer to God.

Date _____ Key Verse–Source _____

What I Am Learning

My Response

Date _____ Key Verse–Source _____

What I Am Learning

My Response

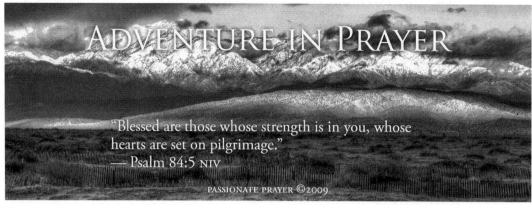

ADVENTURE IN PRAYER

"Blessed are those whose strength is in you, whose hearts are set on pilgrimage."
— Psalm 84:5 NIV

PASSIONATE PRAYER ©2009

Record your journey by writing what you are learning about prayer. Include date, key scripture & sources, and respond in prayer to God.

Date _____ Key Verse–Source _____

What I Am Learning

My Response

Date _____ Key Verse–Source _____

What I Am Learning

My Response

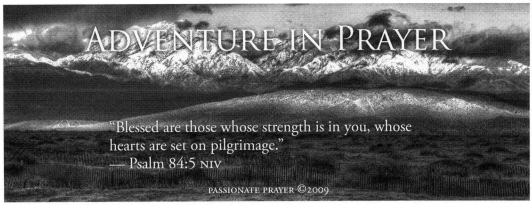

ADVENTURE IN PRAYER

"Blessed are those whose strength is in you, whose
hearts are set on pilgrimage."
— Psalm 84:5 NIV

Record your journey by writing what you are learning about prayer. Include date, key scripture &
sources, and respond in prayer to God.

Date _____ Key Verse–Source _____

What I Am Learning

My Response

Date _____ Key Verse–Source _____

What I Am Learning

My Response

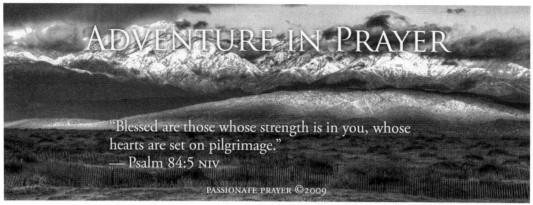

Adventure in Prayer

"Blessed are those whose strength is in you, whose
hearts are set on pilgrimage."
— Psalm 84:5 NIV

PASSIONATE PRAYER ©2009

*Record your journey by writing what you are learning about prayer. Include date, key scripture &
sources, and respond in prayer to God.*

Date _____ Key Verse–Source _____

What I Am Learning

My Response

Date _____ Key Verse–Source _____

What I Am Learning

My Response

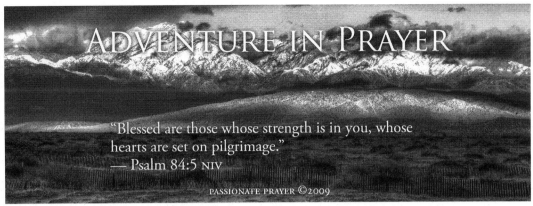

ADVENTURE IN PRAYER

"Blessed are those whose strength is in you, whose hearts are set on pilgrimage."
— Psalm 84:5 NIV

PASSIONATE PRAYER ©2009

Record your journey by writing what you are learning about prayer. Include date, key scripture & sources, and respond in prayer to God.

Date _____ *Key Verse–Source* _____

What I Am Learning

My Response

Date _____ *Key Verse–Source* _____

What I Am Learning

My Response

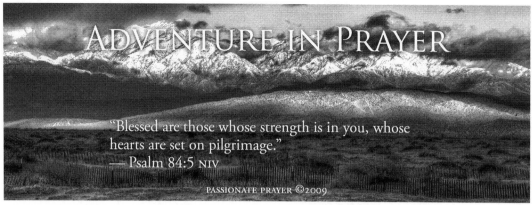

ADVENTURE IN PRAYER

"Blessed are those whose strength is in you, whose
hearts are set on pilgrimage."
— Psalm 84:5 NIV

PASSIONATE PRAYER ©2009

Record your journey by writing what you are learning about prayer. Include date, key scripture &
sources, and respond in prayer to God.

Date _____ Key Verse–Source _____

What I Am Learning

My Response

Date _____ Key Verse–Source _____

What I Am Learning

My Response

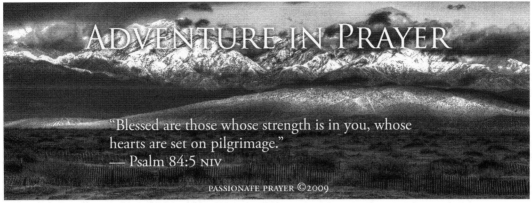

ADVENTURE IN PRAYER

"Blessed are those whose strength is in you, whose
hearts are set on pilgrimage."
— Psalm 84:5 NIV

PASSIONATE PRAYER ©2009

Record your journey by writing what you are learning about prayer. Include date, key scripture &
sources, and respond in prayer to God.

Date _____ Key Verse–Source _____

What I Am Learning

My Response

Date _____ Key Verse–Source _____

What I Am Learning

My Response

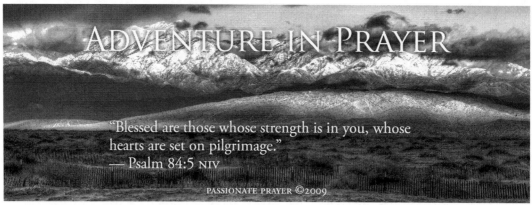

Adventure in Prayer

"Blessed are those whose strength is in you, whose hearts are set on pilgrimage."
— Psalm 84:5 NIV

PASSIONATE PRAYER ©2009

Record your journey by writing what you are learning about prayer. Include date, key scripture & sources, and respond in prayer to God.

Date _____ Key Verse–Source _____

What I Am Learning

My Response

Date _____ Key Verse–Source _____

What I Am Learning

My Response

ADVENTURE IN PRAYER

"Blessed are those whose strength is in you, whose hearts are set on pilgrimage."
— Psalm 84:5 NIV

PASSIONATE PRAYER ©2009

Record your journey by writing what you are learning about prayer. Include date, key scripture & sources, and respond in prayer to God.

Date _____ *Key Verse–Source* _____

What I Am Learning

My Response

Date _____ *Key Verse–Source* _____

What I Am Learning

My Response

ADVENTURE IN PRAYER

"Blessed are those whose strength is in you, whose hearts are set on pilgrimage."
— Psalm 84:5 NIV

PASSIONATE PRAYER ©2009

Record your journey by writing what you are learning about prayer. Include date, key scripture & sources, and respond in prayer to God.

Date _____ Key Verse–Source _____

What I Am Learning

My Response

Date _____ Key Verse–Source _____

What I Am Learning

My Response

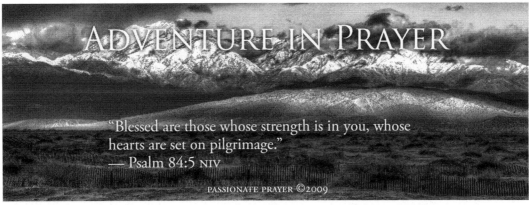

ADVENTURE IN PRAYER

"Blessed are those whose strength is in you, whose hearts are set on pilgrimage."
— Psalm 84:5 NIV

PASSIONATE PRAYER ©2009

Record your journey by writing what you are learning about prayer. Include date, key scripture & sources, and respond in prayer to God.

Date _____ *Key Verse–Source* _____

What I Am Learning

My Response

Date _____ *Key Verse–Source* _____

What I Am Learning

My Response

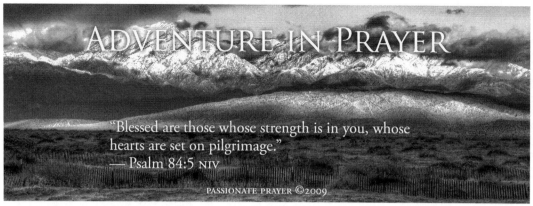

ADVENTURE IN PRAYER

"Blessed are those whose strength is in you, whose hearts are set on pilgrimage."
— Psalm 84:5 NIV

PASSIONATE PRAYER ©2009

Record your journey by writing what you are learning about prayer. Include date, key scripture & sources, and respond in prayer to God.

Date _____ Key Verse–Source _____

What I Am Learning

My Response

Date _____ Key Verse–Source _____

What I Am Learning

My Response

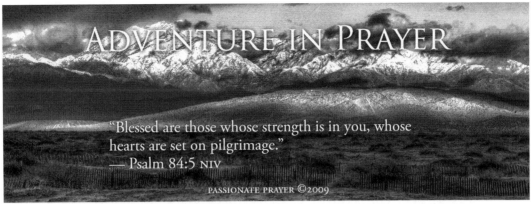

ADVENTURE IN PRAYER

"Blessed are those whose strength is in you, whose hearts are set on pilgrimage."
— Psalm 84:5 NIV

PASSIONATE PRAYER ©2009

Record your journey by writing what you are learning about prayer. Include date, key scripture & sources, and respond in prayer to God.

Date _____ *Key Verse–Source* _____

What I Am Learning

My Response

Date _____ *Key Verse–Source* _____

What I Am Learning

My Response

ADVENTURE IN PRAYER

"Blessed are those whose strength is in you, whose hearts are set on pilgrimage."
— Psalm 84:5 NIV

PASSIONATE PRAYER ©2009

Record your journey by writing what you are learning about prayer. Include date, key scripture & sources, and respond in prayer to God.

Date _____ Key Verse–Source _____

What I Am Learning

My Response

Date _____ Key Verse–Source _____

What I Am Learning

My Response

ADVENTURE IN PRAYER

"Blessed are those whose strength is in you, whose hearts are set on pilgrimage."
— Psalm 84:5 NIV

PASSIONATE PRAYER ©2009

Record your journey by writing what you are learning about prayer. Include date, key scripture & sources, and respond in prayer to God.

Date _____ *Key Verse–Source* _____

What I Am Learning

My Response

Date _____ *Key Verse–Source* _____

What I Am Learning

My Response

ADVENTURE IN PRAYER

"Blessed are those whose strength is in you, whose hearts are set on pilgrimage."
— Psalm 84:5 NIV

Record your journey by writing what you are learning about prayer. Include date, key scripture & sources, and respond in prayer to God.

Date _____ Key Verse–Source _____

What I Am Learning

My Response

Date _____ Key Verse–Source _____

What I Am Learning

My Response

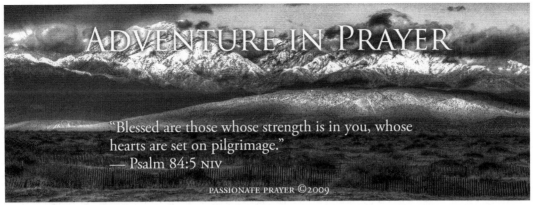

ADVENTURE IN PRAYER

"Blessed are those whose strength is in you, whose
hearts are set on pilgrimage."
— Psalm 84:5 NIV

Record your journey by writing what you are learning about prayer. Include date, key scripture &
sources, and respond in prayer to God.

Date _____ Key Verse–Source _____

What I Am Learning

My Response

Date _____ Key Verse–Source _____

What I Am Learning

My Response

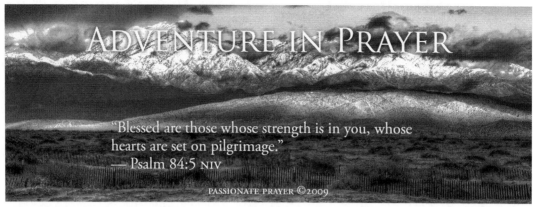

ADVENTURE IN PRAYER

"Blessed are those whose strength is in you, whose hearts are set on pilgrimage."
— Psalm 84:5 NIV

PASSIONATE PRAYER ©2009

Record your journey by writing what you are learning about prayer. Include date, key scripture & sources, and respond in prayer to God.

Date _____ *Key Verse–Source* _____

What I Am Learning

My Response

Date _____ *Key Verse–Source* _____

What I Am Learning

My Response

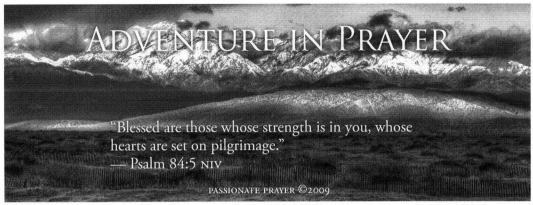

ADVENTURE IN PRAYER

"Blessed are those whose strength is in you, whose hearts are set on pilgrimage."
— Psalm 84:5 NIV

PASSIONATE PRAYER ©2009

Record your journey by writing what you are learning about prayer. Include date, key scripture & sources, and respond in prayer to God.

Date _____ Key Verse–Source _____

What I Am Learning

My Response

Date _____ Key Verse–Source _____

What I Am Learning

My Response

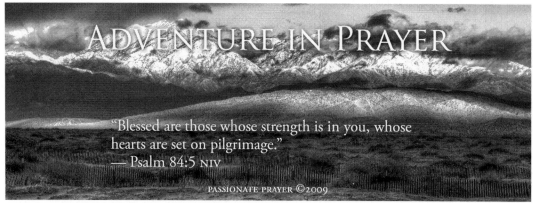

ADVENTURE IN PRAYER

"Blessed are those whose strength is in you, whose hearts are set on pilgrimage."
— Psalm 84:5 NIV

PASSIONATE PRAYER ©2009

Record your journey by writing what you are learning about prayer. Include date, key scripture & sources, and respond in prayer to God.

Date _____ Key Verse–Source _____

What I Am Learning

My Response

Date _____ Key Verse–Source _____

What I Am Learning

My Response

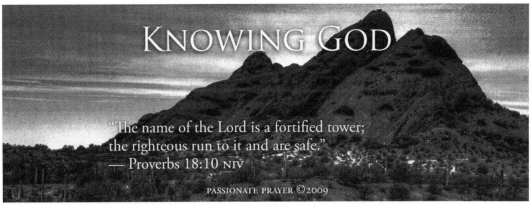

KNOWING GOD

"The name of the Lord is a fortified tower;
the righteous run to it and are safe."
— Proverbs 18:10 NIV

PASSIONATE PRAYER ©2009

The goal in prayer, as in all of life, is to know God. As you study God's Word and pray, write what you learn when God shows you a truth about Himself.

Date _____ *Key Verse–Source* _____

What I Am Learning

My Response

Date _____ *Key Verse–Source* _____

What I Am Learning

My Response

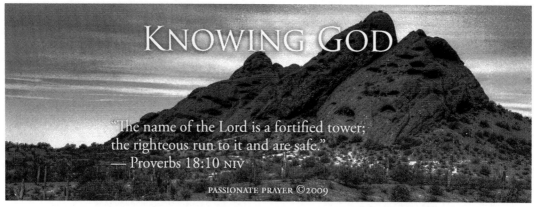

KNOWING GOD

*"The name of the Lord is a fortified tower;
the righteous run to it and are safe."*
— Proverbs 18:10 NIV

PASSIONATE PRAYER ©2009

The goal in prayer, as in all of life, is to know God. As you study God's Word and pray, write what you learn when God shows you a truth about Himself.

Date _____ Key Verse–Source _____

What I Am Learning

My Response

Date _____ Key Verse–Source _____

What I Am Learning

My Response

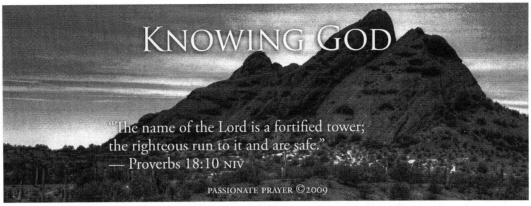

KNOWING GOD

"The name of the Lord is a fortified tower;
the righteous run to it and are safe."
— Proverbs 18:10 NIV

PASSIONATE PRAYER ©2009

The goal in prayer, as in all of life, is to know God. As you study God's Word and pray, write what you learn when God shows you a truth about Himself.

Date _____ Key Verse–Source _____

What I Am Learning

My Response

Date _____ Key Verse–Source _____

What I Am Learning

My Response

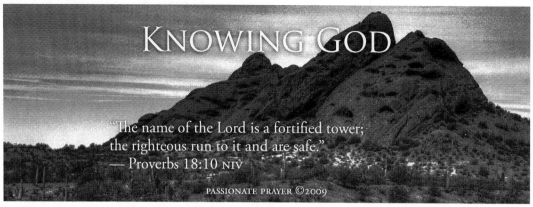

KNOWING GOD

"The name of the Lord is a fortified tower;
the righteous run to it and are safe."
— Proverbs 18:10 NIV

PASSIONATE PRAYER ©2009

The goal in prayer, as in all of life, is to know God. As you study God's Word and pray, write what you learn when God shows you a truth about Himself.

Date _____ Key Verse–Source _____

What I Am Learning

My Response

Date _____ Key Verse–Source _____

What I Am Learning

My Response

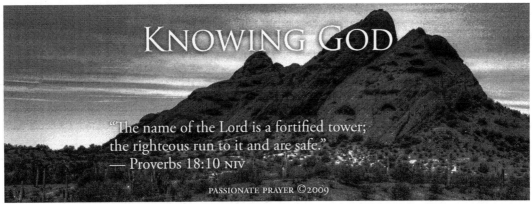

KNOWING GOD

"The name of the Lord is a fortified tower;
the righteous run to it and are safe."
— Proverbs 18:10 NIV

PASSIONATE PRAYER ©2009

The goal in prayer, as in all of life, is to know God. As you study God's Word and pray, write what you learn when God shows you a truth about Himself.

Date _____ *Key Verse–Source* _____

What I Am Learning

My Response

Date _____ *Key Verse–Source* _____

What I Am Learning

My Response

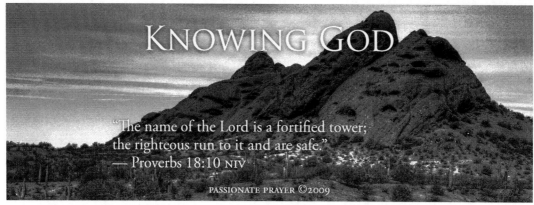

KNOWING GOD

"The name of the Lord is a fortified tower;
the righteous run to it and are safe."
— Proverbs 18:10 NIV

PASSIONATE PRAYER ©2009

The goal in prayer, as in all of life, is to know God. As you study God's Word and pray, write what you learn when God shows you a truth about Himself.

Date _____ *Key Verse–Source* _____

What I Am Learning

My Response

Date _____ *Key Verse–Source* _____

What I Am Learning

My Response

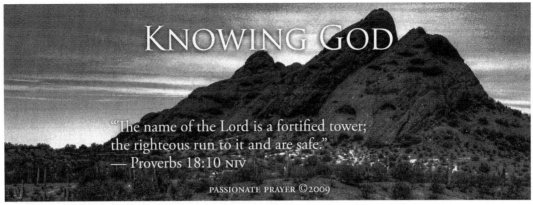

KNOWING GOD

"The name of the Lord is a fortified tower;
the righteous run to it and are safe."
— Proverbs 18:10 NIV

PASSIONATE PRAYER ©2009

The goal in prayer, as in all of life, is to know God. As you study God's Word and pray, write what you learn when God shows you a truth about Himself.

Date _____ Key Verse–Source _____

What I Am Learning

My Response

Date _____ Key Verse–Source _____

What I Am Learning

My Response

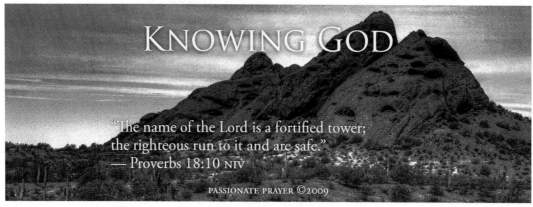

KNOWING GOD

"The name of the Lord is a fortified tower;
the righteous run to it and are safe."
— Proverbs 18:10 NIV

PASSIONATE PRAYER ©2009

The goal in prayer, as in all of life, is to know God. As you study God's Word and pray, write what you learn when God shows you a truth about Himself.

Date _____ Key Verse–Source _____

What I Am Learning

My Response

Date _____ Key Verse–Source _____

What I Am Learning

My Response

KNOWING GOD

"The name of the Lord is a fortified tower;
the righteous run to it and are safe."
— Proverbs 18:10 NIV

PASSIONATE PRAYER ©2009

The goal in prayer, as in all of life, is to know God. As you study God's Word and pray, write what you learn when God shows you a truth about Himself.

Date _____ *Key Verse–Source* _____

What I Am Learning

My Response

Date _____ *Key Verse–Source* _____

What I Am Learning

My Response

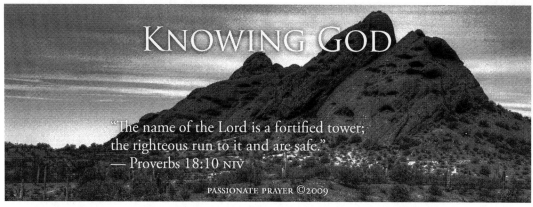

KNOWING GOD

"The name of the Lord is a fortified tower;
the righteous run to it and are safe."
— Proverbs 18:10 NIV

PASSIONATE PRAYER ©2009

The goal in prayer, as in all of life, is to know God. As you study God's Word and pray, write what you learn when God shows you a truth about Himself.

Date _____ Key Verse–Source _____

What I Am Learning

My Response

Date _____ Key Verse–Source _____

What I Am Learning

My Response

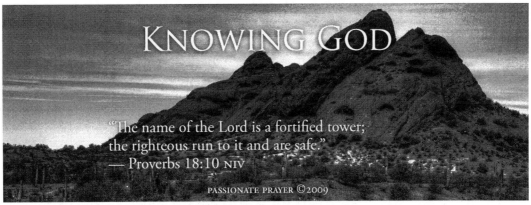

KNOWING GOD

*"The name of the Lord is a fortified tower;
the righteous run to it and are safe."*
— Proverbs 18:10 NIV

PASSIONATE PRAYER © 2009

The goal in prayer, as in all of life, is to know God. As you study God's Word and pray, write what you learn when God shows you a truth about Himself.

Date _____ Key Verse–Source _____

What I Am Learning

My Response

Date _____ Key Verse–Source _____

What I Am Learning

My Response

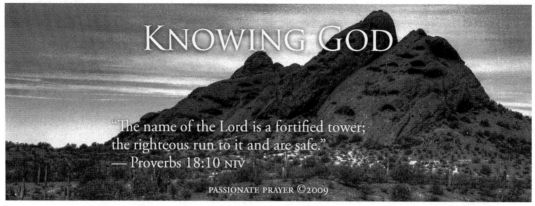

KNOWING GOD

"The name of the Lord is a fortified tower;
the righteous run to it and are safe."
— Proverbs 18:10 NIV

PASSIONATE PRAYER ©2009

The goal in prayer, as in all of life, is to know God. As you study God's Word and pray, write what you learn when God shows you a truth about Himself.

Date _____ Key Verse–Source _____

What I Am Learning

My Response

Date _____ Key Verse–Source _____

What I Am Learning

My Response

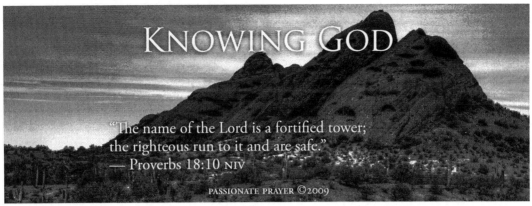

KNOWING GOD

"The name of the Lord is a fortified tower;
the righteous run to it and are safe."
— Proverbs 18:10 NIV

PASSIONATE PRAYER ©2009

The goal in prayer, as in all of life, is to know God. As you study God's Word and pray, write what you learn when God shows you a truth about Himself.

Date _____ *Key Verse–Source* _____

What I Am Learning

My Response

Date _____ *Key Verse–Source* _____

What I Am Learning

My Response

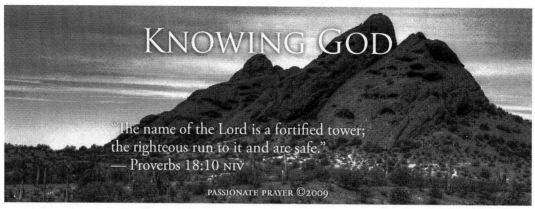

KNOWING GOD

"The name of the Lord is a fortified tower;
the righteous run to it and are safe."
— Proverbs 18:10 NIV

PASSIONATE PRAYER ©2009

The goal in prayer, as in all of life, is to know God. As you study God's Word and pray, write what you learn when God shows you a truth about Himself.

Date _____ *Key Verse–Source* _____

What I Am Learning

My Response

Date _____ *Key Verse–Source* _____

What I Am Learning

My Response

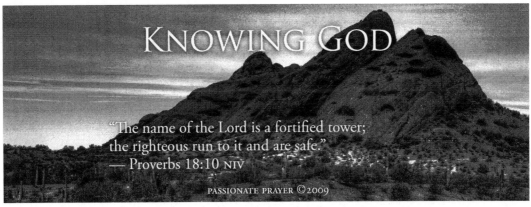

KNOWING GOD

"The name of the Lord is a fortified tower; the righteous run to it and are safe."
— Proverbs 18:10 NIV

PASSIONATE PRAYER ©2009

The goal in prayer, as in all of life, is to know God. As you study God's Word and pray, write what you learn when God shows you a truth about Himself.

Date _____ Key Verse–Source _____

What I Am Learning

My Response

Date _____ Key Verse–Source _____

What I Am Learning

My Response

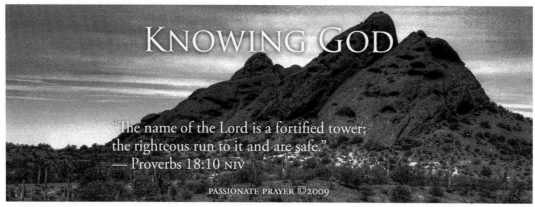

The goal in prayer, as in all of life, is to know God. As you study God's Word and pray, write what you learn when God shows you a truth about Himself.

Date _____ Key Verse–Source _____

What I Am Learning

My Response

Date _____ Key Verse–Source _____

What I Am Learning

My Response

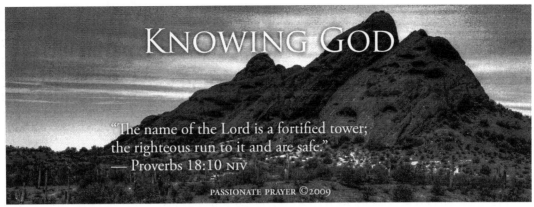

KNOWING GOD

"The name of the Lord is a fortified tower;
the righteous run to it and are safe."
— Proverbs 18:10 NIV

PASSIONATE PRAYER ©2009

The goal in prayer, as in all of life, is to know God. As you study God's Word and pray, write what you learn when God shows you a truth about Himself.

Date _____ Key Verse–Source _____

What I Am Learning

My Response

Date _____ Key Verse–Source _____

What I Am Learning

My Response

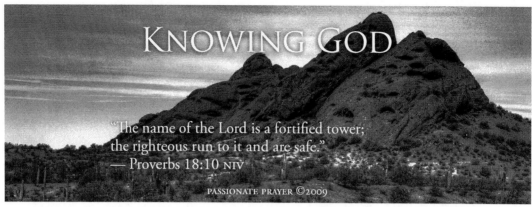

KNOWING GOD

"The name of the Lord is a fortified tower;
the righteous run to it and are safe."
— Proverbs 18:10 NIV

PASSIONATE PRAYER ©2009

The goal in prayer, as in all of life, is to know God. As you study God's Word and pray, write what you learn when God shows you a truth about Himself.

Date _____ Key Verse–Source _____

What I Am Learning

My Response

Date _____ Key Verse–Source _____

What I Am Learning

My Response

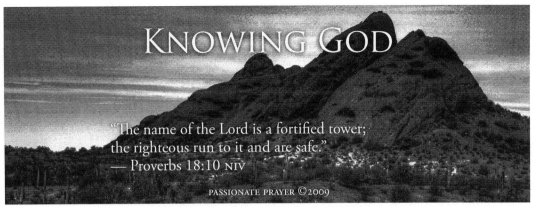

KNOWING GOD

*"The name of the Lord is a fortified tower;
the righteous run to it and are safe."*
— Proverbs 18:10 NIV

PASSIONATE PRAYER ©2009

The goal in prayer, as in all of life, is to know God. As you study God's Word and pray, write what you learn when God shows you a truth about Himself.

Date _____ Key Verse–Source _____

What I Am Learning

My Response

Date _____ Key Verse–Source _____

What I Am Learning

My Response

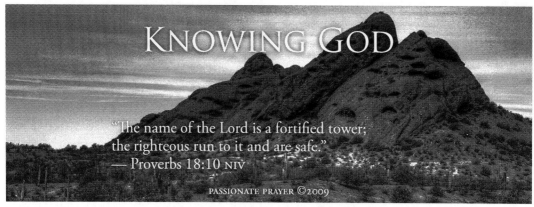

KNOWING GOD

"The name of the Lord is a fortified tower;
the righteous run to it and are safe."
— Proverbs 18:10 NIV

PASSIONATE PRAYER ©2009

The goal in prayer, as in all of life, is to know God. As you study God's Word and pray, write what you learn when God shows you a truth about Himself.

Date _____ *Key Verse–Source* _____

What I Am Learning

My Response

.

Date _____ *Key Verse–Source* _____

What I Am Learning

My Response

KNOWING GOD

"The name of the Lord is a fortified tower;
the righteous run to it and are safe."
— Proverbs 18:10 NIV

PASSIONATE PRAYER ©2009

The goal in prayer, as in all of life, is to know God. As you study God's Word and pray, write what you learn when God shows you a truth about Himself.

Date _____ Key Verse–Source _____

What I Am Learning

My Response

Date _____ Key Verse–Source _____

What I Am Learning

My Response

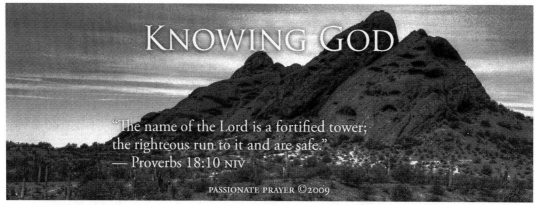

KNOWING GOD

"The name of the Lord is a fortified tower;
the righteous run to it and are safe."
— Proverbs 18:10 NIV

PASSIONATE PRAYER ©2009

The goal in prayer, as in all of life, is to know God. As you study God's Word and pray, write what you learn when God shows you a truth about Himself.

Date _____ *Key Verse–Source* _____

What I Am Learning

My Response

Date _____ *Key Verse–Source* _____

What I Am Learning

My Response

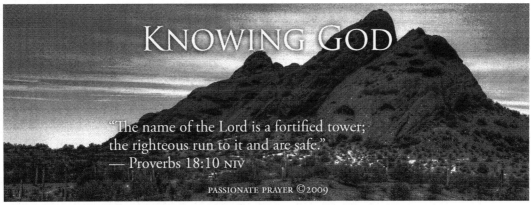

KNOWING GOD

"The name of the Lord is a fortified tower;
the righteous run to it and are safe."
— Proverbs 18:10 NIV

PASSIONATE PRAYER ©2009

The goal in prayer, as in all of life, is to know God. As you study God's Word and pray, write what you learn when God shows you a truth about Himself.

Date _____ *Key Verse–Source* _____

What I Am Learning

My Response

Date _____ *Key Verse–Source* _____

What I Am Learning

My Response

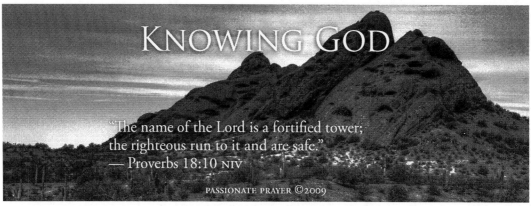

KNOWING GOD

"The name of the Lord is a fortified tower;
the righteous run to it and are safe."
— Proverbs 18:10 NIV

PASSIONATE PRAYER ©2009

The goal in prayer, as in all of life, is to know God. As you study God's Word and pray, write what you learn when God shows you a truth about Himself.

Date _____ Key Verse–Source _____

What I Am Learning

My Response

Date _____ Key Verse–Source _____

What I Am Learning

My Response

KNOWING GOD

*"The name of the Lord is a fortified tower;
the righteous run to it and are safe."*
— Proverbs 18:10 NIV

PASSIONATE PRAYER ©2009

The goal in prayer, as in all of life, is to know God. As you study God's Word and pray, write what you learn when God shows you a truth about Himself.

Date _____ Key Verse–Source _____

What I Am Learning

My Response

Date _____ Key Verse–Source _____

What I Am Learning

My Response

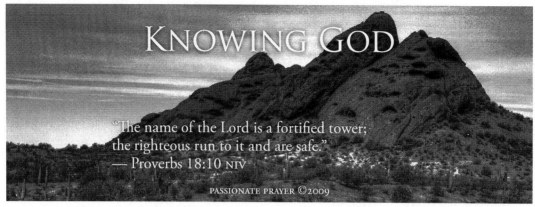

KNOWING GOD

"The name of the Lord is a fortified tower;
the righteous run to it and are safe."
— Proverbs 18:10 NIV

PASSIONATE PRAYER ©2009

The goal in prayer, as in all of life, is to know God. As you study God's Word and pray, write what you learn when God shows you a truth about Himself.

Date _____ Key Verse–Source _____

What I Am Learning

My Response

Date _____ Key Verse–Source _____

What I Am Learning

My Response

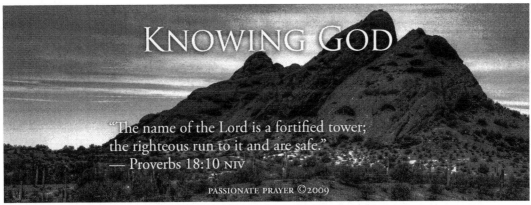

"The name of the Lord is a fortified tower;
the righteous run to it and are safe."
— Proverbs 18:10 NIV

PASSIONATE PRAYER ©2009

The goal in prayer, as in all of life, is to know God. As you study God's Word and pray, write what you learn when God shows you a truth about Himself.

Date _____ Key Verse–Source _____

What I Am Learning

My Response

Date _____ Key Verse–Source _____

What I Am Learning

My Response

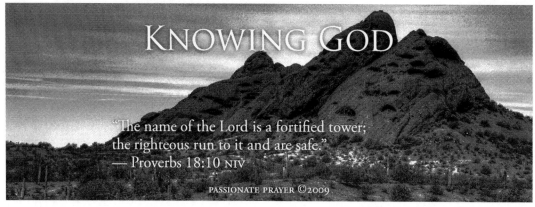

KNOWING GOD

"The name of the Lord is a fortified tower;
the righteous run to it and are safe."
— Proverbs 18:10 NIV

PASSIONATE PRAYER ©2009

The goal in prayer, as in all of life, is to know God. As you study God's Word and pray, write what you learn when God shows you a truth about Himself.

Date _____ *Key Verse–Source* _____

What I Am Learning

My Response

Date _____ *Key Verse–Source* _____

What I Am Learning

My Response

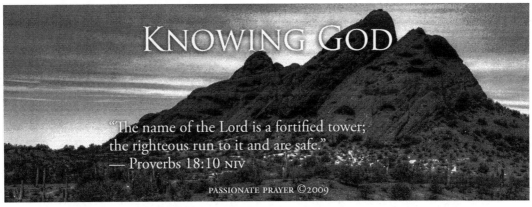

KNOWING GOD

"The name of the Lord is a fortified tower;
the righteous run to it and are safe."
— Proverbs 18:10 NIV

PASSIONATE PRAYER ©2009

The goal in prayer, as in all of life, is to know God. As you study God's Word and pray, write what you learn when God shows you a truth about Himself.

Date _____ *Key Verse–Source* _____

What I Am Learning

My Response

Date _____ *Key Verse–Source* _____

What I Am Learning

My Response

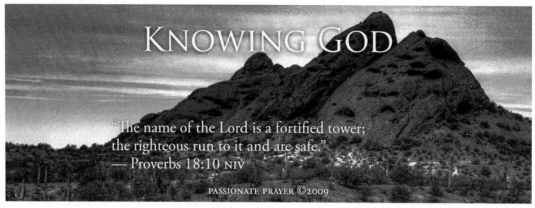

KNOWING GOD

"The name of the Lord is a fortified tower;
the righteous run to it and are safe."
— Proverbs 18:10 NIV

PASSIONATE PRAYER ©2009

The goal in prayer, as in all of life, is to know God. As you study God's Word and pray, write what you learn when God shows you a truth about Himself.

Date _____ Key Verse–Source _____

What I Am Learning

My Response

Date _____ Key Verse–Source _____

What I Am Learning

My Response

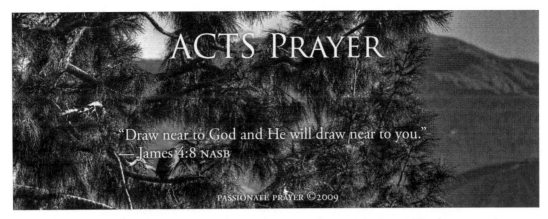

ACTS PRAYER

"Draw near to God and He will draw near to you."
— James 4:8 NASB

PASSIONATE PRAYER ©2009

Write out the prayers on your heart according to ACTS—Adoration, Confession, Thanksgiving, and Supplication. You may want to use Scripture as well as your own words.

Date _____

Adoration

Confession

Thanksgiving

Supplication

Date _____

Adoration

Confession

Thanksgiving

Supplication

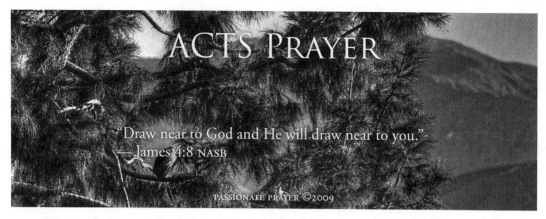

ACTS PRAYER

"Draw near to God and He will draw near to you."
—James 4:8 NASB

PASSIONATE PRAYER ©2009

Write out the prayers on your heart according to ACTS—Adoration, Confession, Thanksgiving, and Supplication. You may want to use Scripture as well as your own words.

Date _____

Adoration

Confession

Thanksgiving

Supplication

Date _____

Adoration

Confession

Thanksgiving

Supplication

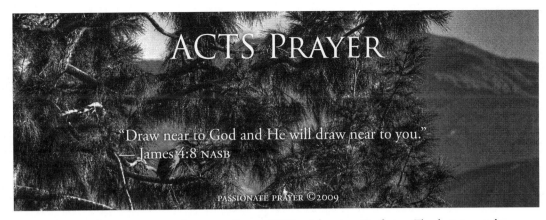

ACTS PRAYER

"Draw near to God and He will draw near to you."
—James 4:8 NASB

PASSIONATE PRAYER ©2009

Write out the prayers on your heart according to ACTS—Adoration, Confession, Thanksgiving, and Supplication. You may want to use Scripture as well as your own words.

Date _____

Adoration

Confession

Thanksgiving

Supplication

Date _____

Adoration

Confession

Thanksgiving

Supplication

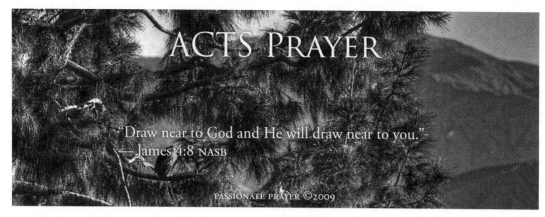

ACTS PRAYER

"Draw near to God and He will draw near to you."
—James 4:8 NASB

Write out the prayers on your heart according to ACTS—Adoration, Confession, Thanksgiving, and Supplication. You may want to use Scripture as well as your own words.

Date _____

Adoration

Confession

Thanksgiving

Supplication

Date _____

Adoration

Confession

Thanksgiving

Supplication

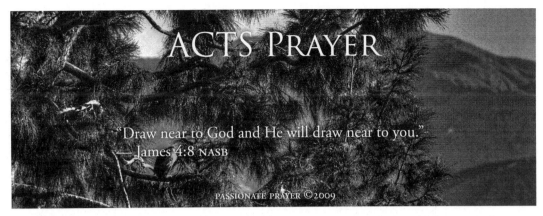

ACTS PRAYER

"Draw near to God and He will draw near to you."
—James 4:8 NASB

PASSIONATE PRAYER ©2009

Write out the prayers on your heart according to ACTS—Adoration, Confession, Thanksgiving, and Supplication. You may want to use Scripture as well as your own words.

Date _____

Adoration

Confession

Thanksgiving

Supplication

Date _____

Adoration

Confession

Thanksgiving

Supplication

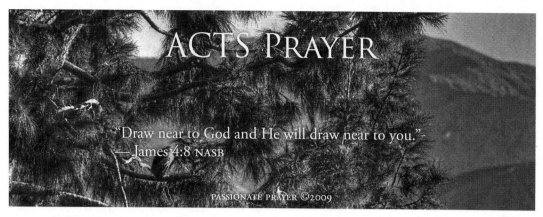

ACTS PRAYER

"Draw near to God and He will draw near to you."
—James 4:8 NASB

Write out the prayers on your heart according to ACTS—Adoration, Confession, Thanksgiving, and Supplication. You may want to use Scripture as well as your own words.

Date _____

Adoration

Confession

Thanksgiving

Supplication

Date _____

Adoration

Confession

Thanksgiving

Supplication

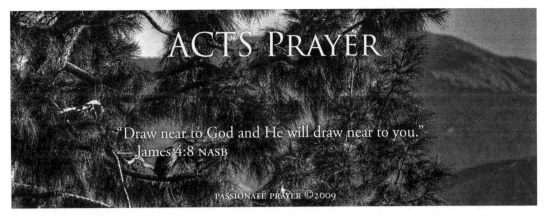

ACTS PRAYER

"Draw near to God and He will draw near to you."
—James 4:8 NASB

PASSIONATE PRAYER ©2009

Write out the prayers on your heart according to ACTS—Adoration, Confession, Thanksgiving, and Supplication. You may want to use Scripture as well as your own words.

Date _____

Adoration

Confession

Thanksgiving

Supplication

Date _____

Adoration

Confession

Thanksgiving

Supplication

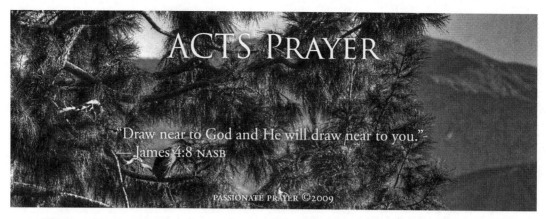

ACTS PRAYER

"Draw near to God and He will draw near to you."
—James 4:8 NASB

Write out the prayers on your heart according to ACTS—Adoration, Confession, Thanksgiving, and Supplication. You may want to use Scripture as well as your own words.

Date _____

Adoration

Confession

Thanksgiving

Supplication

Date _____

Adoration

Confession

Thanksgiving

Supplication

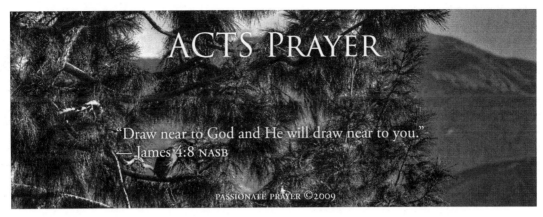

ACTS Prayer

"Draw near to God and He will draw near to you."
—James 4:8 NASB

PASSIONATE PRAYER ©2009

Write out the prayers on your heart according to ACTS—Adoration, Confession, Thanksgiving, and Supplication. You may want to use Scripture as well as your own words.

Date _____

Adoration

Confession

Thanksgiving

Supplication

Date _____

Adoration

Confession

Thanksgiving

Supplication

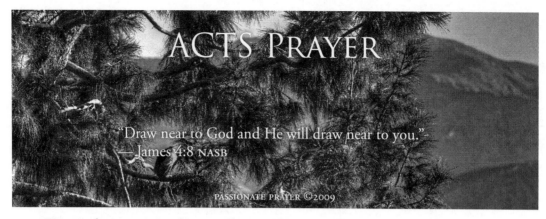

ACTS PRAYER

"Draw near to God and He will draw near to you."–
—James 4:8 NASB

PASSIONATE PRAYER ©2009

Write out the prayers on your heart according to ACTS—Adoration, Confession, Thanksgiving, and Supplication. You may want to use Scripture as well as your own words.

Date _____

Adoration

Confession

Thanksgiving

Supplication

Date _____

Adoration

Confession

Thanksgiving

Supplication

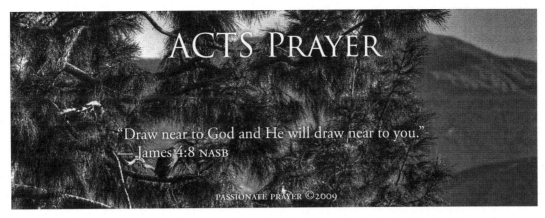

ACTS Prayer

"Draw near to God and He will draw near to you."
— James 4:8 NASB

PASSIONATE PRAYER ©2009

Write out the prayers on your heart according to ACTS—Adoration, Confession, Thanksgiving, and Supplication. You may want to use Scripture as well as your own words.

Date _____

Adoration

Confession

Thanksgiving

Supplication

Date _____

Adoration

Confession

Thanksgiving

Supplication

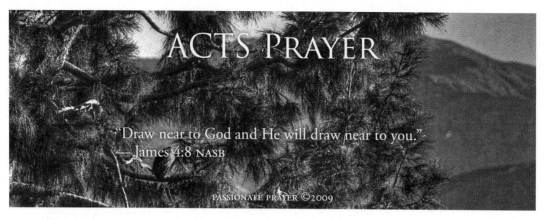

ACTS PRAYER

"Draw near to God and He will draw near to you."
— James 4:8 NASB

Write out the prayers on your heart according to ACTS—Adoration, Confession, Thanksgiving, and Supplication. You may want to use Scripture as well as your own words.

Date _____

Adoration

Confession

Thanksgiving

Supplication

Date _____

Adoration

Confession

Thanksgiving

Supplication

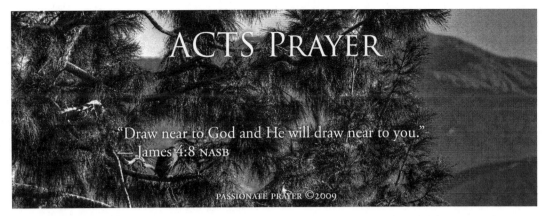

ACTS PRAYER

"Draw near to God and He will draw near to you."
— James 4:8 NASB

PASSIONATE PRAYER ©2009

Write out the prayers on your heart according to ACTS—Adoration, Confession, Thanksgiving, and Supplication. You may want to use Scripture as well as your own words.

Date _____

Adoration

Confession

Thanksgiving

Supplication

Date _____

Adoration

Confession

Thanksgiving

Supplication

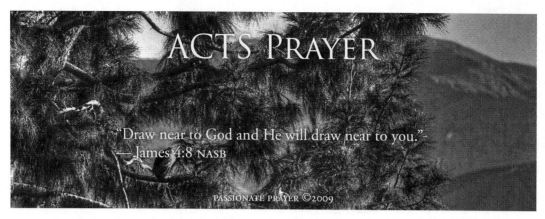

ACTS PRAYER

"Draw near to God and He will draw near to you."
—James 4:8 NASB

PASSIONATE PRAYER ©2009

Write out the prayers on your heart according to ACTS—Adoration, Confession, Thanksgiving, and Supplication. You may want to use Scripture as well as your own words.

Date _____

Adoration

Confession

Thanksgiving

Supplication

Date _____

Adoration

Confession

Thanksgiving

Supplication

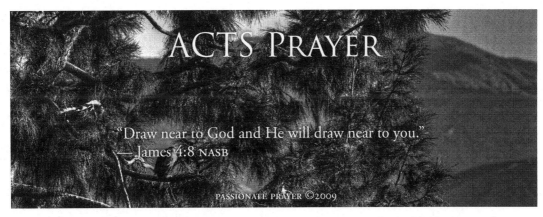

ACTS PRAYER

"Draw near to God and He will draw near to you."
— James 4:8 NASB

PASSIONATE PRAYER ©2009

Write out the prayers on your heart according to ACTS—Adoration, Confession, Thanksgiving, and Supplication. You may want to use Scripture as well as your own words.

Date _____

Adoration

Confession

Thanksgiving

Supplication

Date _____

Adoration

Confession

Thanksgiving

Supplication

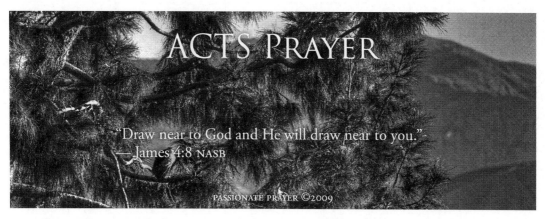

ACTS PRAYER

"Draw near to God and He will draw near to you."-
—James 4:8 NASB

PASSIONATE PRAYER ©2009

Write out the prayers on your heart according to ACTS—Adoration, Confession, Thanksgiving, and Supplication. You may want to use Scripture as well as your own words.

Date _____

Adoration

Confession

Thanksgiving

Supplication

Date _____

Adoration

Confession

Thanksgiving

Supplication

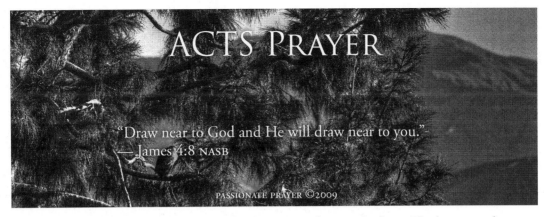

ACTS PRAYER

"Draw near to God and He will draw near to you."
—James 4:8 NASB

PASSIONATE PRAYER ©2009

Write out the prayers on your heart according to ACTS—Adoration, Confession, Thanksgiving, and Supplication. You may want to use Scripture as well as your own words.

Date _____

Adoration

Confession

Thanksgiving

Supplication

Date _____

Adoration

Confession

Thanksgiving

Supplication

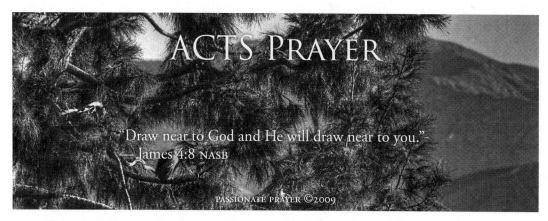

ACTS PRAYER

"Draw near to God and He will draw near to you."
—James 4:8 NASB

Write out the prayers on your heart according to ACTS—Adoration, Confession, Thanksgiving, and Supplication. You may want to use Scripture as well as your own words.

Date _____

Adoration

Confession

Thanksgiving

Supplication

Date _____

Adoration

Confession

Thanksgiving

Supplication

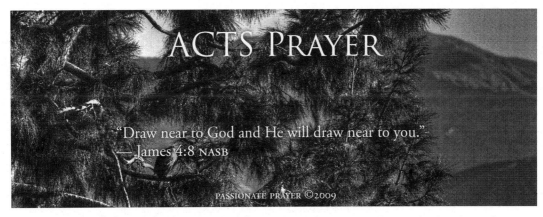

ACTS PRAYER

"Draw near to God and He will draw near to you."
— James 4:8 NASB

Write out the prayers on your heart according to ACTS—Adoration, Confession, Thanksgiving, and Supplication. You may want to use Scripture as well as your own words.

Date _____

Adoration

Confession

Thanksgiving

Supplication

Date _____

Adoration

Confession

Thanksgiving

Supplication

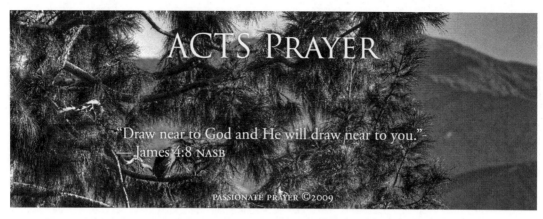

ACTS PRAYER

"Draw near to God and He will draw near to you."
—James 4:8 NASB

PASSIONATE PRAYER ©2009

Write out the prayers on your heart according to ACTS—Adoration, Confession, Thanksgiving, and Supplication. You may want to use Scripture as well as your own words.

Date _____

Adoration

Confession

Thanksgiving

Supplication

Date _____

Adoration

Confession

Thanksgiving

Supplication

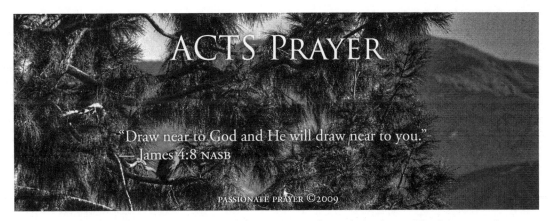

ACTS PRAYER

"Draw near to God and He will draw near to you."
— James 4:8 NASB

PASSIONATE PRAYER ©2009

Write out the prayers on your heart according to ACTS—Adoration, Confession, Thanksgiving, and Supplication. You may want to use Scripture as well as your own words.

Date _____

Adoration

Confession

Thanksgiving

Supplication

Date _____

Adoration

Confession

Thanksgiving

Supplication

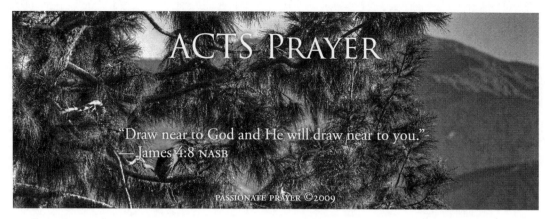

ACTS PRAYER

"Draw near to God and He will draw near to you."
—James 4:8 NASB

Write out the prayers on your heart according to ACTS—Adoration, Confession, Thanksgiving, and Supplication. You may want to use Scripture as well as your own words.

Date _____

Adoration

Confession

Thanksgiving

Supplication

Date _____

Adoration

Confession

Thanksgiving

Supplication

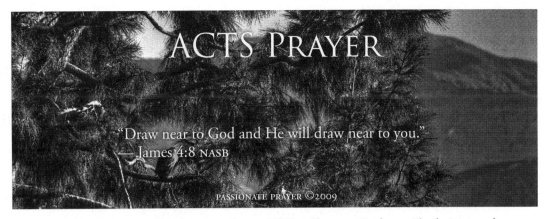

ACTS PRAYER

"Draw near to God and He will draw near to you."
—James 4:8 NASB

PASSIONATE PRAYER ©2009

Write out the prayers on your heart according to ACTS—Adoration, Confession, Thanksgiving, and Supplication. You may want to use Scripture as well as your own words.

Date _____

Adoration

Confession

Thanksgiving

Supplication

Date _____

Adoration

Confession

Thanksgiving

Supplication

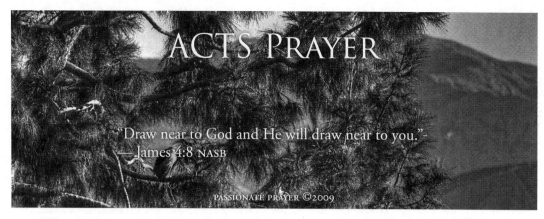

ACTS PRAYER

"Draw near to God and He will draw near to you."
—James 4:8 NASB

PASSIONATE PRAYER ©2009

Write out the prayers on your heart according to ACTS—Adoration, Confession, Thanksgiving, and Supplication. You may want to use Scripture as well as your own words.

Date _____

Adoration

Confession

Thanksgiving

Supplication

Date _____

Adoration

Confession

Thanksgiving

Supplication

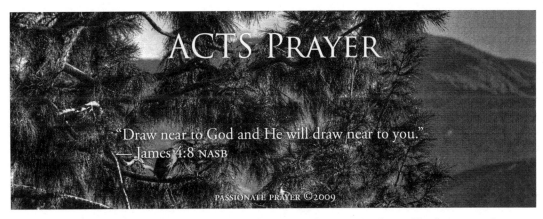

ACTS PRAYER

"Draw near to God and He will draw near to you."
—James 4:8 NASB

PASSIONATE PRAYER ©2009

Write out the prayers on your heart according to ACTS—Adoration, Confession, Thanksgiving, and Supplication. You may want to use Scripture as well as your own words.

Date _____

Adoration

Confession

Thanksgiving

Supplication

Date _____

Adoration

Confession

Thanksgiving

Supplication

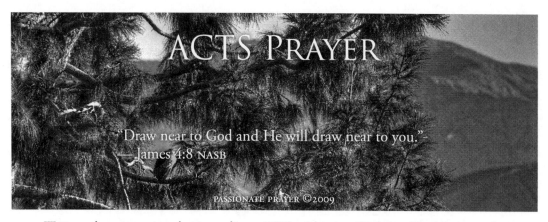

ACTS PRAYER

"Draw near to God and He will draw near to you."
—James 4:8 NASB

PASSIONATE PRAYER ©2009

Write out the prayers on your heart according to ACTS—Adoration, Confession, Thanksgiving, and Supplication. You may want to use Scripture as well as your own words.

Date _____

Adoration

Confession

Thanksgiving

Supplication

Date _____

Adoration

Confession

Thanksgiving

Supplication

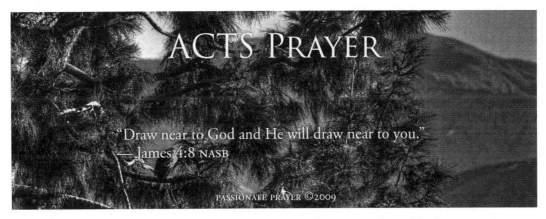

ACTS PRAYER

"Draw near to God and He will draw near to you."
— James 4:8 NASB

PASSIONATE PRAYER ©2009

Write out the prayers on your heart according to ACTS—Adoration, Confession, Thanksgiving, and Supplication. You may want to use Scripture as well as your own words.

Date _____

Adoration

Confession

Thanksgiving

Supplication

Date _____

Adoration

Confession

Thanksgiving

Supplication

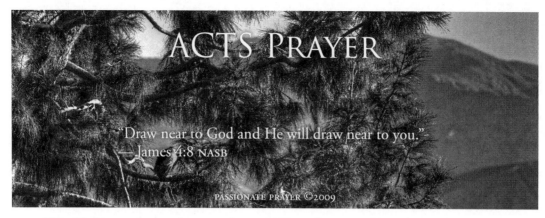

ACTS PRAYER

"Draw near to God and He will draw near to you."
—James 4:8 NASB

Write out the prayers on your heart according to ACTS—Adoration, Confession, Thanksgiving, and Supplication. You may want to use Scripture as well as your own words.

Date _____

Adoration

Confession

Thanksgiving

Supplication

Date _____

Adoration

Confession

Thanksgiving

Supplication

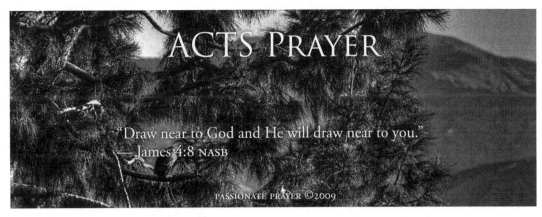

ACTS PRAYER

"Draw near to God and He will draw near to you."
—James 4:8 NASB

PASSIONATE PRAYER ©2009

Write out the prayers on your heart according to ACTS—Adoration, Confession, Thanksgiving, and Supplication. You may want to use Scripture as well as your own words.

Date _____

Adoration

Confession

Thanksgiving

Supplication

Date _____

Adoration

Confession

Thanksgiving

Supplication

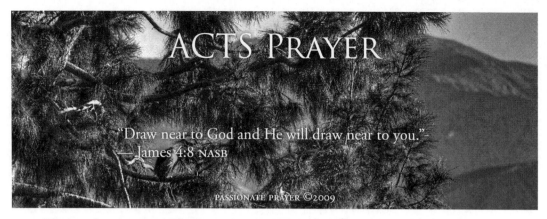

ACTS PRAYER

"Draw near to God and He will draw near to you."
—James 4:8 NASB

PASSIONATE PRAYER ©2009

Write out the prayers on your heart according to ACTS—Adoration, Confession, Thanksgiving, and Supplication. You may want to use Scripture as well as your own words.

Date _____

Adoration

Confession

Thanksgiving

Supplication

Date _____

Adoration

Confession

Thanksgiving

Supplication

PRAYER FOCUS

"The prayer of a righteous person is powerful and effective." — James 5:16 TNIV

PASSIONATE PRAYER ©2009

Write out your top prayers, requests, and answers to prayer for a selected period of time—every month, week, or day. You may want to use the daily focus to enhance your prayer time. Daily Focus: Sunday—church, pastors, leaders, Monday—nation, Tuesday—world, Wednesday—community, Thursday—missionaries and ministries, Friday—your ministry, Saturday—revival

My Prayers   *Dates–Month, Week, Day*_____

God's Answers

What I'm Learning

PRAYER FOCUS

"The prayer of a righteous person is powerful and effective." — James 5:16 TNIV

PASSIONATE PRAYER ©2009

Write out your top prayers, requests, and answers to prayer for a selected period of time—every month, week, or day. You may want to use the daily focus to enhance your prayer time. Daily Focus: Sunday—church, pastors, leaders, Monday—nation, Tuesday—world, Wednesday—community, Thursday—missionaries and ministries, Friday—your ministry, Saturday—revival

My Prayers　　　　*Dates—Month, Week, Day*_____

God's Answers

What I'm Learning

PRAYER FOCUS

"The prayer of a righteous person is powerful and effective." —James 5:16 TNIV

PASSIONATE PRAYER ©2009

Write out your top prayers, requests, and answers to prayer for a selected period of time—every month, week, or day. You may want to use the daily focus to enhance your prayer time. Daily Focus: Sunday— church, pastors, leaders, Monday—nation, Tuesday—world, Wednesday—community, Thursday— missionaries and ministries, Friday—your ministry, Saturday—revival

My Prayers   *Dates—Month, Week, Day*_____

God's Answers

What I'm Learning

PRAYER FOCUS

"The prayer of a righteous person is powerful and effective." — James 5:16 TNIV

PASSIONATE PRAYER ©2009

Write out your top prayers, requests, and answers to prayer for a selected period of time—every month, week, or day. You may want to use the daily focus to enhance your prayer time. Daily Focus: Sunday—church, pastors, leaders, Monday—nation, Tuesday—world, Wednesday—community, Thursday—missionaries and ministries, Friday—your ministry, Saturday—revival

My Prayers   *Dates–Month, Week, Day*_____

God's Answers

What I'm Learning

PRAYER FOCUS

"The prayer of a righteous person is powerful and effective." —James 5:16 TNIV

PASSIONATE PRAYER ©2009

Write out your top prayers, requests, and answers to prayer for a selected period of time—every month, week, or day. You may want to use the daily focus to enhance your prayer time. Daily Focus: Sunday—church, pastors, leaders, Monday—nation, Tuesday—world, Wednesday—community, Thursday—missionaries and ministries, Friday—your ministry, Saturday—revival

My Prayers   *Dates—Month, Week, Day*_____

God's Answers

What I'm Learning

PRAYER FOCUS

"The prayer of a righteous person is powerful and effective." —James 5:16 TNIV

PASSIONATE PRAYER ©2009

Write out your top prayers, requests, and answers to prayer for a selected period of time—every month, week, or day. You may want to use the daily focus to enhance your prayer time. Daily Focus: Sunday—church, pastors, leaders, Monday—nation, Tuesday—world, Wednesday—community, Thursday—missionaries and ministries, Friday—your ministry, Saturday—revival

My Prayers   *Dates–Month, Week, Day*_____

God's Answers

What I'm Learning

PRAYER FOCUS

"The prayer of a righteous person is powerful and effective." —James 5:16 TNIV

PASSIONATE PRAYER ©2009

Write out your top prayers, requests, and answers to prayer for a selected period of time—every month, week, or day. You may want to use the daily focus to enhance your prayer time. Daily Focus: Sunday—church, pastors, leaders, Monday—nation, Tuesday—world, Wednesday—community, Thursday—missionaries and ministries, Friday—your ministry, Saturday—revival

My Prayers   *Dates—Month, Week, Day*_____

God's Answers

What I'm Learning

PRAYER FOCUS

"The prayer of a righteous person is powerful and effective." — James 5:16 TNIV

PASSIONATE PRAYER ©2009

Write out your top prayers, requests, and answers to prayer for a selected period of time—every month, week, or day. You may want to use the daily focus to enhance your prayer time. Daily Focus: Sunday— church, pastors, leaders, Monday—nation, Tuesday—world, Wednesday—community, Thursday— missionaries and ministries, Friday—your ministry, Saturday—revival

My Prayers   *Dates–Month, Week, Day*_____

God's Answers

What I'm Learning

PRAYER FOCUS

"The prayer of a righteous person is powerful and effective." —James 5:16 TNIV

PASSIONATE PRAYER ©2009

Write out your top prayers, requests, and answers to prayer for a selected period of time—every month, week, or day. You may want to use the daily focus to enhance your prayer time. Daily Focus: Sunday—church, pastors, leaders, Monday—nation, Tuesday—world, Wednesday—community, Thursday—missionaries and ministries, Friday—your ministry, Saturday—revival

My Prayers   *Dates–Month, Week, Day*_____

God's Answers

What I'm Learning

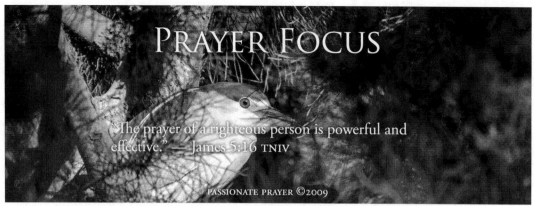

PRAYER FOCUS

"The prayer of a righteous person is powerful and effective." — James 5:16 TNIV

PASSIONATE PRAYER ©2009

Write out your top prayers, requests, and answers to prayer for a selected period of time—every month, week, or day. You may want to use the daily focus to enhance your prayer time. Daily Focus: Sunday—church, pastors, leaders, Monday—nation, Tuesday—world, Wednesday—community, Thursday—missionaries and ministries, Friday—your ministry, Saturday—revival

My Prayers   *Dates–Month, Week, Day*_____

God's Answers

What I'm Learning

PRAYER FOCUS

"The prayer of a righteous person is powerful and effective." — James 5:16 TNIV

PASSIONATE PRAYER ©2009

Write out your top prayers, requests, and answers to prayer for a selected period of time—every month, week, or day. You may want to use the daily focus to enhance your prayer time. Daily Focus: Sunday—church, pastors, leaders, Monday—nation, Tuesday—world, Wednesday—community, Thursday—missionaries and ministries, Friday—your ministry, Saturday—revival

My Prayers   *Dates—Month, Week, Day*_____

God's Answers

What I'm Learning

PRAYER FOCUS

"The prayer of a righteous person is powerful and effective." — James 5:16 TNIV

PASSIONATE PRAYER ©2009

Write out your top prayers, requests, and answers to prayer for a selected period of time—every month, week, or day. You may want to use the daily focus to enhance your prayer time. Daily Focus: Sunday—church, pastors, leaders, Monday—nation, Tuesday—world, Wednesday—community, Thursday—missionaries and ministries, Friday—your ministry, Saturday—revival

My Prayers   *Dates–Month, Week, Day*_____

God's Answers

What I'm Learning

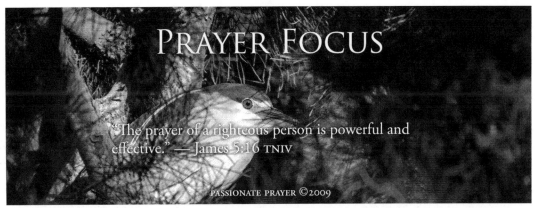

PRAYER FOCUS

"The prayer of a righteous person is powerful and effective." — James 5:16 TNIV

PASSIONATE PRAYER ©2009

Write out your top prayers, requests, and answers to prayer for a selected period of time—every month, week, or day. You may want to use the daily focus to enhance your prayer time. Daily Focus: Sunday—church, pastors, leaders, Monday—nation, Tuesday—world, Wednesday—community, Thursday—missionaries and ministries, Friday—your ministry, Saturday—revival

My Prayers   *Dates—Month, Week, Day*_____

God's Answers

What I'm Learning

PRAYER FOCUS

"The prayer of a righteous person is powerful and effective." — James 5:16 TNIV

PASSIONATE PRAYER ©2009

Write out your top prayers, requests, and answers to prayer for a selected period of time—every month, week, or day. You may want to use the daily focus to enhance your prayer time. Daily Focus: Sunday—church, pastors, leaders, Monday—nation, Tuesday—world, Wednesday—community, Thursday—missionaries and ministries, Friday—your ministry, Saturday—revival

My Prayers   *Dates–Month, Week, Day*_____

God's Answers

What I'm Learning

PRAYER FOCUS

"The prayer of a righteous person is powerful and effective." — James 5:16 TNIV

PASSIONATE PRAYER ©2009

Write out your top prayers, requests, and answers to prayer for a selected period of time—every month, week, or day. You may want to use the daily focus to enhance your prayer time. Daily Focus: Sunday—church, pastors, leaders, Monday—nation, Tuesday—world, Wednesday—community, Thursday—missionaries and ministries, Friday—your ministry, Saturday—revival

My Prayers   *Dates—Month, Week, Day*_____

God's Answers

What I'm Learning

PRAYER FOCUS

"The prayer of a righteous person is powerful and effective." — James 5:16 TNIV

Write out your top prayers, requests, and answers to prayer for a selected period of time—every month, week, or day. You may want to use the daily focus to enhance your prayer time. Daily Focus: Sunday—church, pastors, leaders, Monday—nation, Tuesday—world, Wednesday—community, Thursday—missionaries and ministries, Friday—your ministry, Saturday—revival

My Prayers   *Dates–Month, Week, Day*_____

God's Answers

What I'm Learning

PRAYER FOCUS

"The prayer of a righteous person is powerful and effective." — James 5:16 TNIV

PASSIONATE PRAYER ©2009

Write out your top prayers, requests, and answers to prayer for a selected period of time—every month, week, or day. You may want to use the daily focus to enhance your prayer time. Daily Focus: Sunday— church, pastors, leaders, Monday—nation, Tuesday—world, Wednesday—community, Thursday— missionaries and ministries, Friday—your ministry, Saturday—revival

My Prayers   *Dates–Month, Week, Day*_____

God's Answers

What I'm Learning

PRAYER FOCUS

"The prayer of a righteous person is powerful and effective." — James 5:16 TNIV

PASSIONATE PRAYER ©2009

Write out your top prayers, requests, and answers to prayer for a selected period of time—every month, week, or day. You may want to use the daily focus to enhance your prayer time. Daily Focus: Sunday—church, pastors, leaders, Monday—nation, Tuesday—world, Wednesday—community, Thursday—missionaries and ministries, Friday—your ministry, Saturday—revival

My Prayers   *Dates–Month, Week, Day*_____

God's Answers

What I'm Learning

PRAYER FOCUS

"The prayer of a righteous person is powerful and effective." — James 5:16 TNIV

PASSIONATE PRAYER ©2009

Write out your top prayers, requests, and answers to prayer for a selected period of time—every month, week, or day. You may want to use the daily focus to enhance your prayer time. Daily Focus: Sunday—church, pastors, leaders, Monday—nation, Tuesday—world, Wednesday—community, Thursday—missionaries and ministries, Friday—your ministry, Saturday—revival

My Prayers   Dates–Month, Week, Day_____

God's Answers

What I'm Learning

PRAYER FOCUS

"The prayer of a righteous person is powerful and effective." — James 5:16 TNIV

Write out your top prayers, requests, and answers to prayer for a selected period of time—every month, week, or day. You may want to use the daily focus to enhance your prayer time. Daily Focus: Sunday—church, pastors, leaders, Monday—nation, Tuesday—world, Wednesday—community, Thursday—missionaries and ministries, Friday—your ministry, Saturday—revival

My Prayers   *Dates–Month, Week, Day*_____

God's Answers

What I'm Learning

PRAYER FOCUS

"The prayer of a righteous person is powerful and effective." —James 5:16 TNIV

PASSIONATE PRAYER ©2009

Write out your top prayers, requests, and answers to prayer for a selected period of time—every month, week, or day. You may want to use the daily focus to enhance your prayer time. Daily Focus: Sunday—church, pastors, leaders, Monday—nation, Tuesday—world, Wednesday—community, Thursday—missionaries and ministries, Friday—your ministry, Saturday—revival

My Prayers   *Dates—Month, Week, Day*_____

God's Answers

What I'm Learning

PRAYER FOCUS

"The prayer of a righteous person is powerful and effective." — James 5:16 TNIV

PASSIONATE PRAYER ©2009

Write out your top prayers, requests, and answers to prayer for a selected period of time—every month, week, or day. You may want to use the daily focus to enhance your prayer time. Daily Focus: Sunday—church, pastors, leaders, Monday—nation, Tuesday—world, Wednesday—community, Thursday—missionaries and ministries, Friday—your ministry, Saturday—revival

My Prayers   *Dates–Month, Week, Day*_____

God's Answers

What I'm Learning

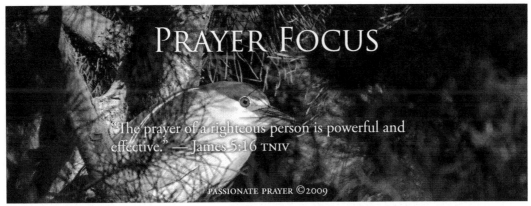

PRAYER FOCUS

"The prayer of a righteous person is powerful and effective." —James 5:16 TNIV

PASSIONATE PRAYER ©2009

Write out your top prayers, requests, and answers to prayer for a selected period of time—every month, week, or day. You may want to use the daily focus to enhance your prayer time. Daily Focus: Sunday— church, pastors, leaders, Monday—nation, Tuesday—world, Wednesday—community, Thursday— missionaries and ministries, Friday—your ministry, Saturday—revival

My Prayers   *Dates—Month, Week, Day*_____

God's Answers

What I'm Learning

PRAYER FOCUS

"The prayer of a righteous person is powerful and effective." —James 5:16 TNIV

PASSIONATE PRAYER ©2009

Write out your top prayers, requests, and answers to prayer for a selected period of time—every month, week, or day. You may want to use the daily focus to enhance your prayer time. Daily Focus: Sunday— church, pastors, leaders, Monday—nation, Tuesday—world, Wednesday—community, Thursday— missionaries and ministries, Friday—your ministry, Saturday—revival

My Prayers   Dates–Month, Week, Day_____

God's Answers

What I'm Learning

PRAYER FOCUS

"The prayer of a righteous person is powerful and effective." —James 5:16 TNIV

PASSIONATE PRAYER ©2009

Write out your top prayers, requests, and answers to prayer for a selected period of time—every month, week, or day. You may want to use the daily focus to enhance your prayer time. Daily Focus: Sunday— church, pastors, leaders, Monday—nation, Tuesday—world, Wednesday—community, Thursday— missionaries and ministries, Friday—your ministry, Saturday—revival

My Prayers   *Dates—Month, Week, Day*_____

God's Answers

What I'm Learning

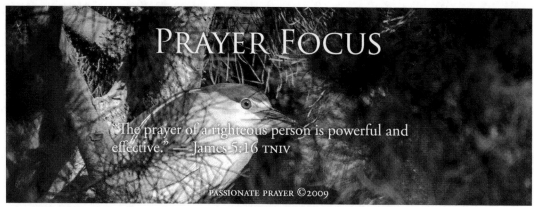

PRAYER FOCUS

"The prayer of a righteous person is powerful and effective." —James 5:16 TNIV

PASSIONATE PRAYER ©2009

Write out your top prayers, requests, and answers to prayer for a selected period of time—every month, week, or day. You may want to use the daily focus to enhance your prayer time. Daily Focus: Sunday—church, pastors, leaders, Monday—nation, Tuesday—world, Wednesday—community, Thursday—missionaries and ministries, Friday—your ministry, Saturday—revival

My Prayers   *Dates–Month, Week, Day*_____

God's Answers

What I'm Learning

PRAYER FOCUS

"The prayer of a righteous person is powerful and effective." — James 5:16 TNIV

PASSIONATE PRAYER ©2009

Write out your top prayers, requests, and answers to prayer for a selected period of time—every month, week, or day. You may want to use the daily focus to enhance your prayer time. Daily Focus: Sunday— church, pastors, leaders, Monday—nation, Tuesday—world, Wednesday—community, Thursday— missionaries and ministries, Friday—your ministry, Saturday—revival

My Prayers   Dates–Month, Week, Day_____

God's Answers

What I'm Learning

PRAYER FOCUS

"The prayer of a righteous person is powerful and effective." — James 5:16 TNIV

PASSIONATE PRAYER ©2009

Write out your top prayers, requests, and answers to prayer for a selected period of time—every month, week, or day. You may want to use the daily focus to enhance your prayer time. Daily Focus: Sunday—church, pastors, leaders, Monday—nation, Tuesday—world, Wednesday—community, Thursday—missionaries and ministries, Friday—your ministry, Saturday—revival

My Prayers   *Dates–Month, Week, Day*_____

God's Answers

What I'm Learning

PRAYER FOCUS

"The prayer of a righteous person is powerful and effective." — James 5:16 TNIV

PASSIONATE PRAYER ©2009

Write out your top prayers, requests, and answers to prayer for a selected period of time—every month, week, or day. You may want to use the daily focus to enhance your prayer time. Daily Focus: Sunday— church, pastors, leaders, Monday—nation, Tuesday—world, Wednesday—community, Thursday— missionaries and ministries, Friday—your ministry, Saturday—revival

My Prayers   *Dates—Month, Week, Day*_____

God's Answers

What I'm Learning

PRAYER FOCUS

"The prayer of a righteous person is powerful and effective." — James 5:16 TNIV

PASSIONATE PRAYER ©2009

Write out your top prayers, requests, and answers to prayer for a selected period of time—every month, week, or day. You may want to use the daily focus to enhance your prayer time. Daily Focus: Sunday—church, pastors, leaders, Monday—nation, Tuesday—world, Wednesday—community, Thursday—missionaries and ministries, Friday—your ministry, Saturday—revival

My Prayers   *Dates–Month, Week, Day*_____

God's Answers

What I'm Learning

APPENDIX

About Catherine Martin
Notes
Quiet Time Ministries Resources

About the Author

Catherine Martin is a summa cum laude graduate of Bethel Theological Seminary with a Master of Arts degree in Theological Studies. She is founder and president of Quiet Time Ministries, director of women's ministries at Southwest Community Church in Indian Wells, California, and adjunct faculty member of Biola University. She is the author of *Six Secrets to a Powerful Quiet Time, Knowing and Loving the Bible, Walking with the God Who Cares, Set my Heart on Fire, Trusting in the Names of God, Passionate Prayer, Quiet Time Moments for Women,* and *Drawing Strength from the Names of God* published by Harvest House Publishers, and *Pilgrimage of the Heart, Revive My Heart!* and *A Heart That Dances,* published by NavPress. She has also written *The Quiet Time Notebook, A Heart on Fire, A Heart to See Forever,* and *A Heart That Hopes in God,* published by Quiet Time Ministries. She is senior editor for *Enriching Your Quiet Time* quarterly magazine. As a popular speaker at retreats and conferences, Catherine challenges others to seek God and love Him with all of their heart, soul, mind, and strength. For more information about Catherine, visit www.quiettime.org.

About Quiet Time Ministries

Quiet Time Ministries is a nonprofit religious organization under Section 501(c)(3) of the Internal Revenue Code. Cash donations are tax deductible as charitable contributions. We count on prayerful donors like you, partners with Quiet Time Ministries pursuing our goals of the furtherance of the Gospel of Jesus Christ and teaching devotion to God and His Word. Visit us online at www.quiettime.org to view special funding opportunities and current ministry projects. Your prayerful donations bring countless project to life!

Quiet Time Ministries | P.O. Box 14007 | Palm Desert, California 92255
1.800.925.6458 | catherine@quiettime.org | www.quiettime.org

 Notes

INTRODUCTION

1. R.A. Torrey, *How To Pray* (Old Tappan, NJ: Fleming H. Revell Company, 1970) pp. 13.
2. Ibid., p. 23.

CHAPTER 1 PassionatePrayer

1. Chambers, *My Utmost for His Highest.* See the entry for October 17.
2. Quoted in S.D. Gordon, *Quiet Talks on Prayer* (New York: Revell, 1904), 141-46.

CHAPTER 2 PassionatePrayer

1. Quoted in Eugene Peterson, *Under the Unpredictable Plant: An Exploration in Vocational Holiness* (Grand Rapids: Eerdmans, 1992), 72.
2. Ole Hallesby, *Prayer* (Minneapolis: Augsburg Fortress, 1994), 17.

CHAPTER 3 PassionatePrayer

1. R.A. Torrey, *How to Pray* (Chicago: Moody, 2007), 15.
2. To learn about this plan and for more information about how to grow in your quiet time, see my 30-day journey *Six Secrets to a Powerful Quiet Time* (Eugene, OR: Harvest House, 2005).
3. Dietrich Bonhoeffer, *Psalms: The Prayer Book of the Bible* (Minneapolis: Augsburg, 1970), 11-12, 15.
4. Mother Teresa, *A Simple Path* (New York: Random House, 1995), 7.
5. F.B. Meyer, *Devotional Commentary* (Wheaton: Tyndale House, 1989), 552.
6. Corrie ten Boom with John and Elizabeth Sherrill, *The Hiding Place* (Old Tappan: Revell, 1971), 196-99, 208-9.
7. To know God more intimately, you may want to read my 30-day journey *Trusting in the Names of God* and the companion book, *Trusting in the Names of God—A Quiet Time Experience* (Eugene, OR: Harvest House, 2008).

CHAPTER 5 PassionatePrayer

1. Eugene Peterson, *Working the Angles: The Shape of Pastoral Integrity* (Grand Rapids, MI: Eerdmans, 1987), 30-31.
2. Hallesby, *Prayer,* 18.

A 30-DAY JOURNEY

PASSIONATE PRAYER

Discovering the Power
of Talking *with* God

CATHERINE MARTIN

Author of *Trusting in the Names of God*

A Quiet Time
EXPERIENCE

PASSIONATE
PRAYER

EIGHT WEEKS OF GUIDED DEVOTIONS
* Inspirational Readings
* Prayer Starters and Journal Ideas
* Questions for Reflection

CATHERINE MARTIN
Author of *Trusting in the Names of God*

CATHERINE MARTIN

Author of *Six Secrets To A Powerful Quiet Time*

THE QUIET TIME NOTEBOOK

The PRAYER Quiet Time Plan

THE QUIET TIME NOTEBOOK

MARTIN

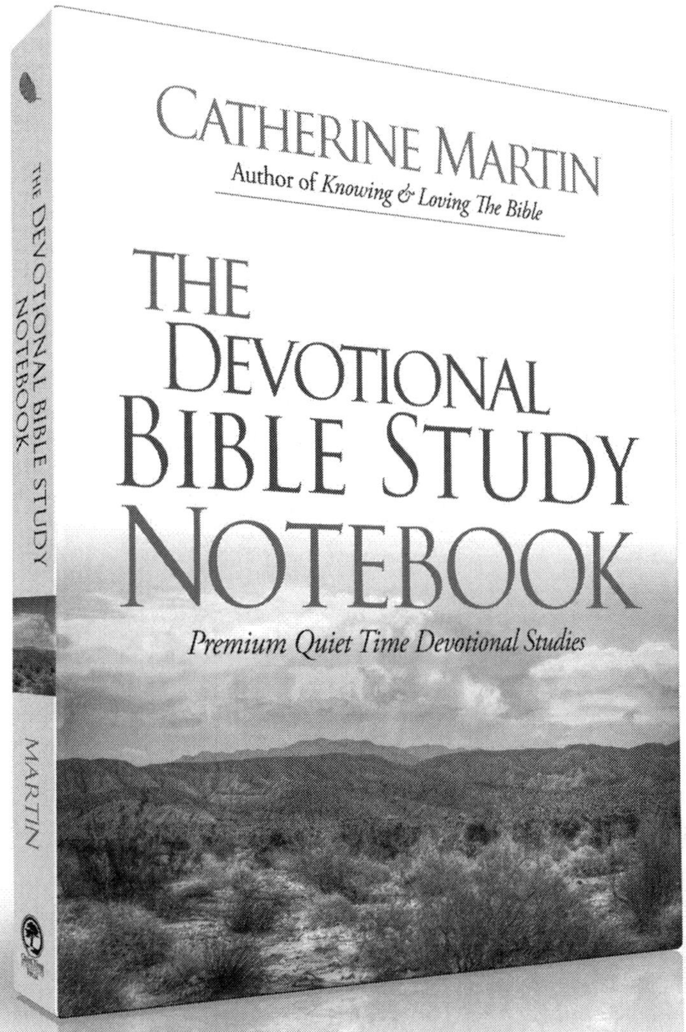

CATHERINE MARTIN

Author of Knowing & Loving The Bible

THE
DEVOTIONAL
BIBLE STUDY
NOTEBOOK

Premium Quiet Time Devotional Studies

THE DEVOTIONAL BIBLE STUDY NOTEBOOK

MARTIN

CATHERINE MARTIN

Author of The Quiet Time Notebook

THE
QUIET TIME
JOURNAL

Pouring Out Your Soul To The Lord